SCIENCE WORKSHOP SERIES
EARTH SCIENCE
The Universe

Seymour Rosen

GLOBE BOOK COMPANY
A Division of Simon & Schuster
Englewood Cliffs, New Jersey

THE AUTHOR

Seymour Rosen received his B.A. and M.S. degrees from Brooklyn College. He taught science in the New York City School System for twenty-seven years. Mr. Rosen was also a contributing participant in a teacher-training program for the development of science curriculum for the New York City Board of Education.

Cover Photograph: Digital Art/Westlight
Photo Researcher: Rhoda Sidney

Photo Credits:

p. 3, Fig. A: New York Public Library
p. 5, Fig. F: NASA
p. 5, Fig. G: NASA
p. 9, Fig. A: The Bettmann Archive
p. 9, Fig. B: Library of Congress
p. 11, Fig. G: National Radio Astronomy Observatory
p. 12: NASA
p. 21, Fig. A: Lick Observatory
p. 31, Fig. D: NASA
p. 35, Fig. A: NOAA/NEDIS/NCDC
p. 35, Fig. B: NASA
p. 35, Fig. C: NASA
p. 35, Fig. D: NASA
p. 35, Fig. E: JPL/NASA
p. 35, Fig. F: NASA
p. 42, Fig. B: NASA
p. 42, Fig. C: NASA
p. 42, Fig. D: NASA
p. 42, Fig. E: NASA
p. 43, Fig. F: NASA
p. 43, Fig. G: NASA
p. 47, Fig. A: NASA
p. 48, Fig. B: NASA
p, 48, Fig. C: NASA
p. 49, Fig. D: NASA
p. 49, Fig. E: NASA
p. 51: NASA
p. 83: Lick Observatory
p. 85, Fig. A: NASA
p. 86, Fig. B: NASA
p. 86, Fig. C: NASA
p. 86, Fig. D: NASA
p. 88, Fig. F: NASA
p. 97: Lick Observatory (all 3 photos)
p. 100, Fig. B: Lick Observatory
p. 100, Fig. C: Lick Observatory

p. 100, Fig. D: Lick Observatory
p. 100, Fig. E: Lick Observatory
p. 100, Fig. G: Lick Observatory
p. 100, Fig. H: Lick Observatory
p. 100, Fig. I: Lick Observatory
p. 103: Lick Observatory
p. 105, Fig. B: Pictorial Parade
p. 106, Fig. C: Lick Observatory
p. 106, Fig. D: UPI/Bettmann Newsphotos
p. 110: American Museum of Natural History
p. 111: Jay Pasachoff
p. 131: Joe Munroe/Photo Researchers
p. 134, Fig. D: NASA
p. 135, Fig. E: NASA
p. 137: NASA (both photos)
p. 139, Fig. A: NASA
p. 140, Fig. B: NASA
p. 141, Fig. C: NASA
p. 142, Fig. D: NASA
p. 142, Fig. E: NASA
p. 145: NASA (all 3 photos)
p. 147, Fig. A: NASA
p. 148, Fig. B: NASA
p. 149, Fig. C: NASA
p. 150, Fig. D: NASA
p. 151, Fig. E: NASA
p. 153: Lick Observatory
p. 162, Fig. D: NASA
p. 162, Fig. E: United Nations/U.S.I.A.
p. 168, Fig. E: Lick Observatory
p. 170: NASA
p. 171: Lick Observatory
p. 173, Fig. A: Lick Observatory
p. 173, Fig. B: Kitt Peak National Observatory
p. 173, Fig. C: Kitt Peak National Observatory
p. 174, Fig. D: Kitt Peak National Observatory

ISBN: 0-8359-0388-5

Printed in the United States of America

8 9 10   99 98

Globe Book Company
A Division of Simon & Schuster
Englewood Cliffs, New Jersey

CONTENTS

Introduction to The Universe

For thousands and thousands of years, humans have watched the sun, moon, stars and planets cross the sky each day and night. They would wonder what these heavenly bodies were and why they behaved the way that they did. Some moved in straight lines while others curved. Some move faster than others.

Today we know much more than the people who watched the sky thousands of years ago. We know that the moon revolves around the earth and that all the planets, including Earth, revolve around the sun.

In this book you will learn about the structure and motions of the planets and much more. You will learn more about the universe than could have been dreamed of a thousand years ago, or even one hundred years ago. Still, there are many things in the universe that we do not yet understand. Today, people still watch the sky and wonder.

Why do we study space?

astronomer [uh-STRON-uh-muhr]:   scientist who studies heavenly bodies
astronomy [uh-STRON-uh-mee]:   study of heavenly bodies
satellite [SAT-uh-lite]:   natural or artificial object orbiting a body in space
universe [YOO-nuh-vurs]:   everything that exists

LESSON 1 | Why do we study space?

Have you ever looked deep into a evening sky? Did you wonder how far away the stars are and what lies beyond the stars. People have always wondered about the heavens. Why?

The answer lies in the natural curiosity of the human mind. We see the sky above us and ask questions. We try to figure out the answers to these questions. However, more often than not, the answers lead to more questions. The study of heavenly bodies is called **astronomy** [uh-STRON-uh-mee]. Scientists who study astronomy are called **astronomers** [uh-STRON-uh-muhrs].

When we study astronomy, we learn a little bit more about the universe. The sun, moon and planets are part of the universe. So are the stars. Everything that exists is part of the universe. So the **universe** [YOO-nuh-vurs] is everything that exists.

Earth is part of the universe. So when we learn more about the universe, we learn more about the earth's place in the universe. For example, the more we learn about the other planets in the solar system, the more we know about planets in general. As we learn more about planets in general, the better we understand the planet earth.

Figure A *Nicholas Copernicus*

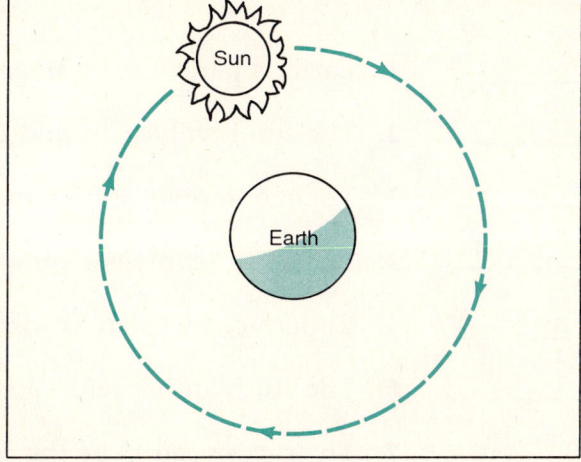

Figure B *People once thought that the sun revolved around the earth.*

For many centuries, people thought that the earth was the center of the universe. They thought that the sun and the stars revolved around the earth. The problem with this explanation was that the planets did not seem to revolve around the earth in any simple way. People made very complex models to try to explain how the planets moved around the earth.

Nicholas Copernicus (koh-PUR-nih-kus) was a Polish astronomer who lived in the 1500s. He studied the sky and made very careful observations even though he had no instruments to help him. Copernicus's studies convinced him that the earth and other planets revolved around the sun. For many years, most people did not believe his ideas. Today we know that they are true.

Copernicus's ideas changed the way humans viewed the universe. We now know that the earth is <u>not</u> the center of the universe but just one small planet among countless stars.

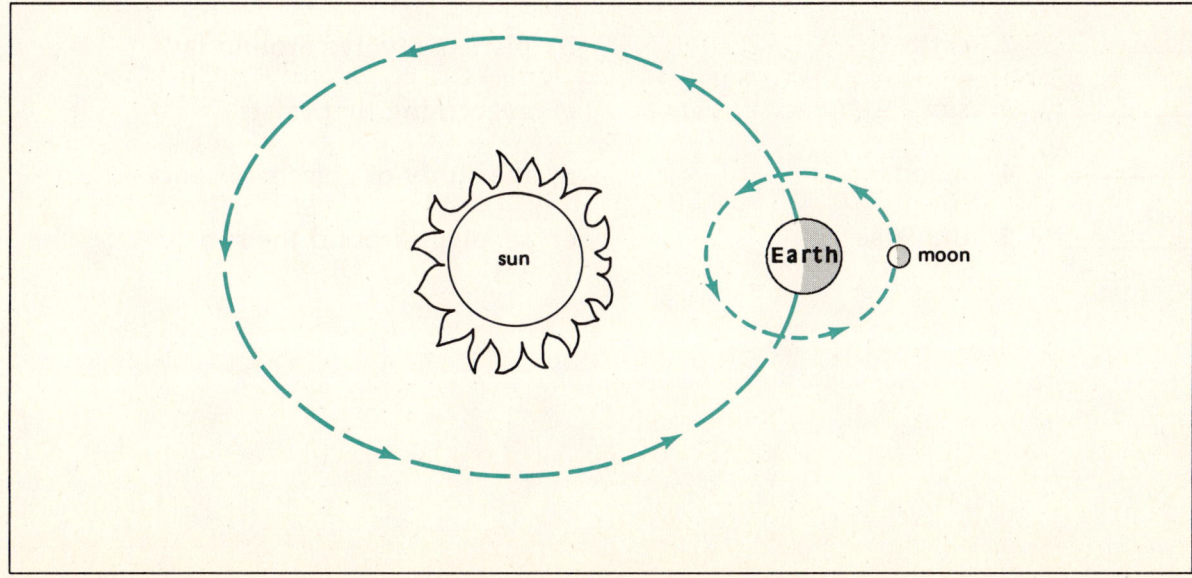

Figure C *We now know that the earth revolves around the sun.*

TRUE OR FALSE

In the space provided, write "true" if the sentence is true. Write "false" if the sentence is false.

_____   **1.** Earth is part of the universe.

_____   **2.** The sun revolves around the earth.

_____   **3.** The moon revolves around the earth.

_____   **4.** The earth revolves around the sun.

_____   **5.** Copernicus was an astronaut.

_____   **6.** The study of heavenly bodies is called astronomy.

_____   **7.** The earth used to be the center of the universe.

_____   **8.** People once that that the earth was the center of the universe.

_____   **9.** Astronomers study astronomy.

_____   **10.** Today, we know everything there is to know about space.

MATCHING

Match each term in Column A with its description in Column B. Write the correct letter in the space provided.

	Column A	**Column B**
_____	**1.** astronomy	**a)** revolves around the earth
_____	**2.** earth	**b)** planets revolve around it
_____	**3.** sun	**c)** everything that exists
_____	**4.** moon	**d)** the study of objects in space
_____	**5.** universe	**e)** revolves around the sun

SPACE EXPLORATION

Scientists do more than study space. They also send things (and people) into space. In 1957, the Soviet Union launched the first artificial satellite, called *Sputnik*, into orbit. Since that time the United States, Soviet Union, and several other countries have launched things into orbit around the Earth. There are a number of reasons to put people and satellites into orbit.

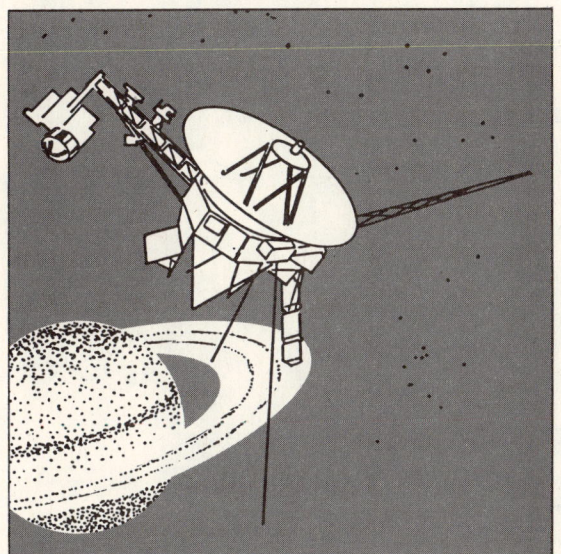

Figure D *Space probes*

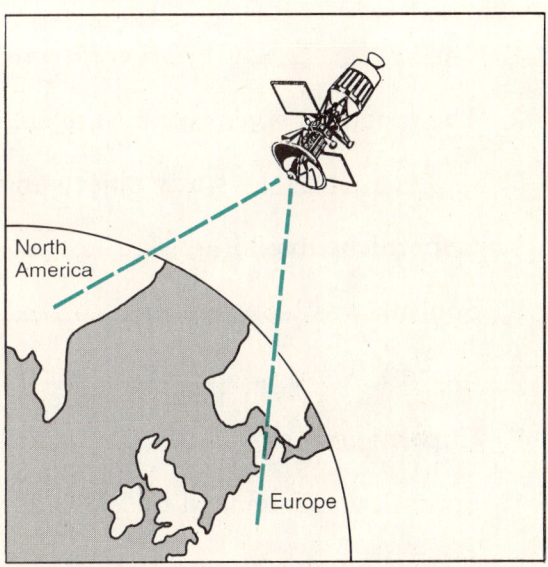

Figure E *Communication satellites*

Figure F *Experiments in zero gravity*

Figure G *Sending people into space*

FILL IN THE BLANK

Complete each statement using a term or terms from the list below. Write your answers in the spaces provided. Some words may be used more than once.

earth	astronomers	1957
sun	the 1500s	satellite
Soviet Union	Polish	

1. The _____ revolves around the _____ .

2. The moon revolves around the _____ .

3. _____ study objects in space.

4. Copernicus lived in _____ .

5. Sputnik was launched in _____ .

6. Sputnik was a _____ .

7. Copernicus was a _____ astronomer.

8. Sputnik was launched by the _____ .

9. Planets revolve around the _____ .

10. Satellites orbit the _____ .

REACHING OUT

Some people believe that society should build places for people to live in space. Why

might people want society to do this. _____

_____

_____

_____

6

What is a telescope?

radio telescope: telescope that can receive radio waves from sources in space
reflecting [rih-FLEKT-ing] **telescope:** telescope that uses a concave mirror to collect light and produce an enlarged image
refracting [rih-FRAKT-ing] **telescope:** telescope that uses convex lenses to collect light and produce an enlarged image
telescope: an instrument that gathers and magnifies light; used to study the heavens

LESSON 2 | What is a telescope?

American astronauts have walked on the moon. But long before they did, telescopes gave us a good idea of what the moon's surface looks like.

You can see the planet Saturn with your eyes alone. But you cannot see its rings. A telescope shows the rings clearly.

Jupiter is visible to the naked eye, too. But you cannot see its moons. Using even a low-power telescope, you can see four of its moons. But with a high-power telescope you can find that there are at least eight more.

There is no questions about it . . . The most useful tool in astronomy is the **telescope**.

There are two main types of telescopes: optical telescopes and the radio telescopes.

OPTICAL TELESCOPES   An optical telescope is an instrument that gathers and magnifies light from faraway places. It makes distant objects seem much larger and closer than they really are.

There are two kinds of optical telescopes:

- A **refracting** [rih-FRAKT-ing] **telescope** uses **lenses** to gather light. A lens is a curved piece of glass. When a beam of light passes through a lens, the light is focused to a single point.

- A **reflecting** [rih-FLEKT-ing] **telescope** uses a curved mirror.

RADIO TELESCOPES   A radio telescope does not gather visible light. Instead, a radio telescope gathers invisible radio energy from objects deep in space. The signals give us clues about the location and makeup of the objects.

Figure A *Hans Lippershey*

Figure B *Galileo*

The optical telescope was invented in 1608 by a Dutch lens maker named Hans Lippershey. Strange as it seems, he was refused a patent.

An Italian astronomer named Galileo made the first practical use of Lippershey's invention. In 1609, Galileo made his first telescope. It was crude and low powered. It enabled him to make important discoveries. Galileo was the first person to see mountains and craters on the moon, the rings of Saturn, and four of Jupiter's moons.

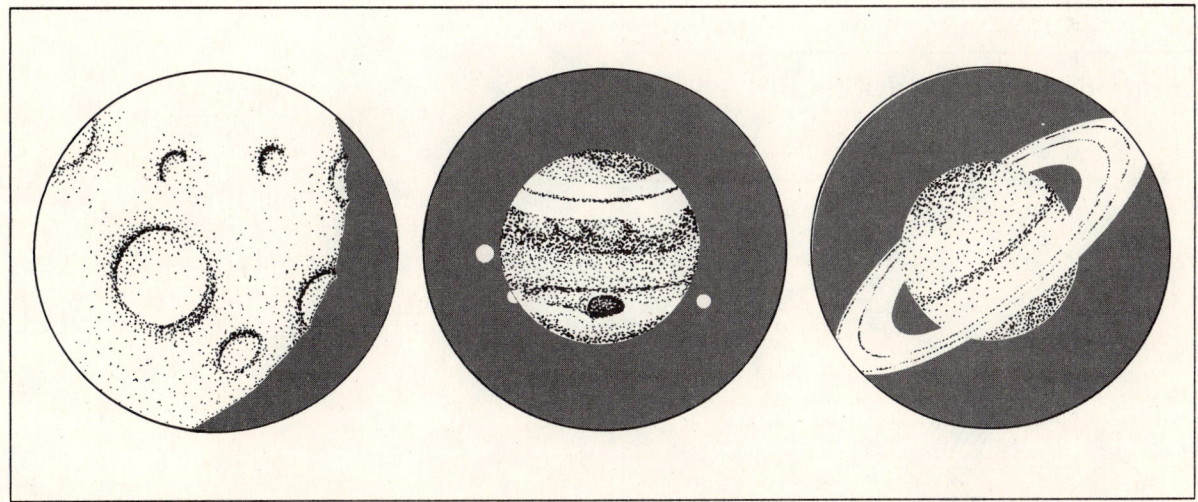

Figure C *Galileo used his telescope to see things that were not visible to the naked eye.*

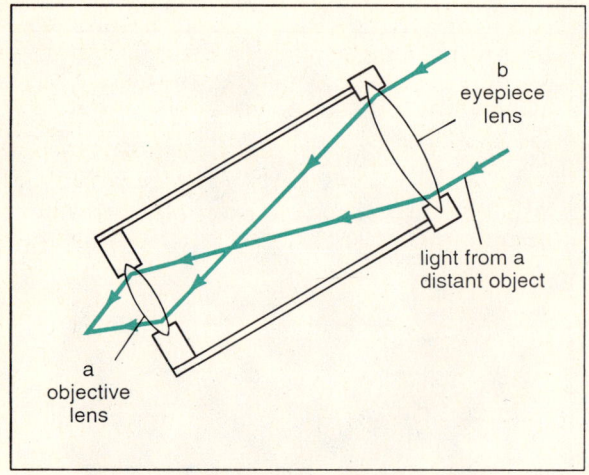

Figure D *Refracting telescope*

Refracting telescopes have two lenses. The objective lens is closer to the object being observed. The eyepiece lens is closer to the eye of the person looking through the telescope.

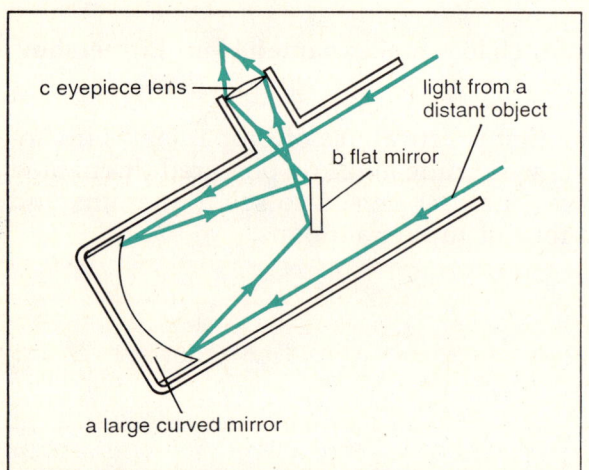

Figure E *Reflecting telescope*

Reflecting telescopes use a curved mirror instead of an objective lens. A curved mirror focuses the light rays the same way that a lens does. A flat mirror is used to change the direction the light is traveling.

Since scientists can make very large mirrors, very large reflecting telescopes can be made. Some telescopes have mirrors that are 4 meters (12 feet) wide.

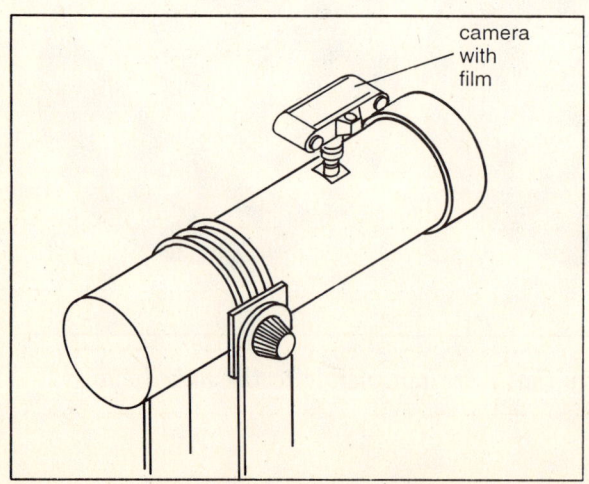

Figure F *Camera attached to a telescope*

Sometimes, a camera is attached to a telescope so that pictures of objects in space can be taken. The camera "looks" through the telescope just as a person would and a picture is taken. The pictures are then studied.

RADIO TELESCOPES

Radio telescopes work like reflecting telescopes. Instead of having a mirror, radio telescopes have large radio dishes. Instead of reflecting visible light, radio dishes reflect radio waves. The radio waves are recorded by a detector into a computer just as light is recorded by a camera onto film.

Figure G   *Radio telescope*

MATCHING

Match each term in Column A with its description in Column B. Write the correct letter in the space provided.

	Column A	Column B
_____	1. reflecting telescope	a) gathers and amplifies radio waves from outer space
_____	2. refracting telescope	b) made first practical use of the telescope
_____	3. radio telescope	c) lens gathers light
_____	4. Lippershey	d) mirror gathers light
_____	5. Galileo	e) invented the optical telescope

REACHING OUT

Galileo made a large number of astronomical discoveries. Why was he able to do this?

_____

_____

_____

SCIENCE *EXTRA*

Hubble Trouble

On April 24, 1990, the Space Shuttle *Discovery* lifted off with the Hubble Space Telescope (HST).

On Earth, telescopes must peer through the atmosphere, which can dim and blur images. The HST was designed to peer into space above Earth's atmosphere. There, HST would be able to see things that could not be seen from the ground. The telescope took years to build and cost 1.6 billion dollars.

During the first few months the HST was in orbit, the telescope's systems were all tested. These tests revealed a horrible and unexpected problem. Images from the telescope were very blurred!

The scientists ran a number of tests to figure out what the problem was. It turned out that the largest mirror in the telescope was the wrong shape.

Making a telescope mirror is a long and complex process. Very complicated devices are used to make sure that the mirror is ground into the proper shape.

When the largest mirror of the HST was made, the main testing device was not working correctly. The mirror was ground into the wrong shape. Tests using other devices hinted that there was something wrong with the mirror. However, the scientists making the mirror assumed that the main testing device was okay and that the other devices were wrong. Even scientists make mistakes.

Now that they know that the mirror is not the right shape, scientists are working on plans to fix the telescope. In 1993, astronauts from the Space Shuttle will repair it.

In addition to the largest mirror, the HST has other smaller mirrors and lenses in it. New mirrors will be made to replace these smaller mirrors in the HST. These new mirrors will be shaped to correct the problems with the main mirror, the way that eye glasses correct blurry vision. These new mirrors and lenses should make the telescope work almost as well as it was designed to.

Meanwhile, some of the experiments the HST was designed to do can still be done with its blurry vision. These experiments will be done until the telescope is repaired. Thus, the situation of the Hubble Space Telescope shows both the capabilities and the limitations of scientists.

What is a spectroscope? 3

spectroscope [SPEK-truh-skohp]: an instrument used to study the light coming from an object
spectrum: bands of different colors of light

LESSON 3 | What is a spectroscope?

Our sun is a star. Everyone knows this now But the early scientists did not believe this. There was no proof! The key to the proof came in 1850 with the invention of the **spectroscope** [SPEK-truh-scohp].

A spectroscope identifies elements by the colors they give off.

Every substance gives off light when it becomes hot enough. Every element gives off its own special color. A spectroscope separates the light into colored lines. We call these lines a **spectrum**. A spectrum is like a fingerprint. No two people have the same fingerprints. And, no two elements have the same spectrum. But the spectrum is always the same for a particular element.

For example:

This is what a sodium spectrum looks like.

yellow bands

Only sodium looks like this. No other elements looks exactly like this.

This is what a boron spectrum looks like.

green bands

Only boron looks like this. No other element looks exactly like this.

There are about 90 natural elements. We know the spectrum for each one. About 67 of them have been found in sunlight. This means that the sun contains at leasts 67 elements that are found on earth.

How do we know that the sun is a star? Simple! The spectroscope patterns of the sun and the stars are very similar.

UNDERSTANDING THE SPECTROSCOPE

The most important part of a spectroscope is a prism. A prism is glass shaped like a wedge. A prism can break up white light into a rainbow of colors.

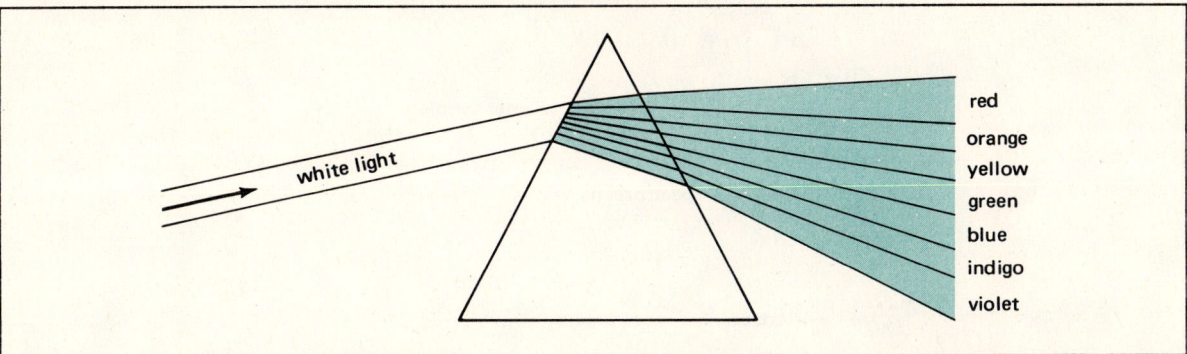

Figure A   *Spectrum of white light.*

HOW A SPECTROSCOPE WORKS

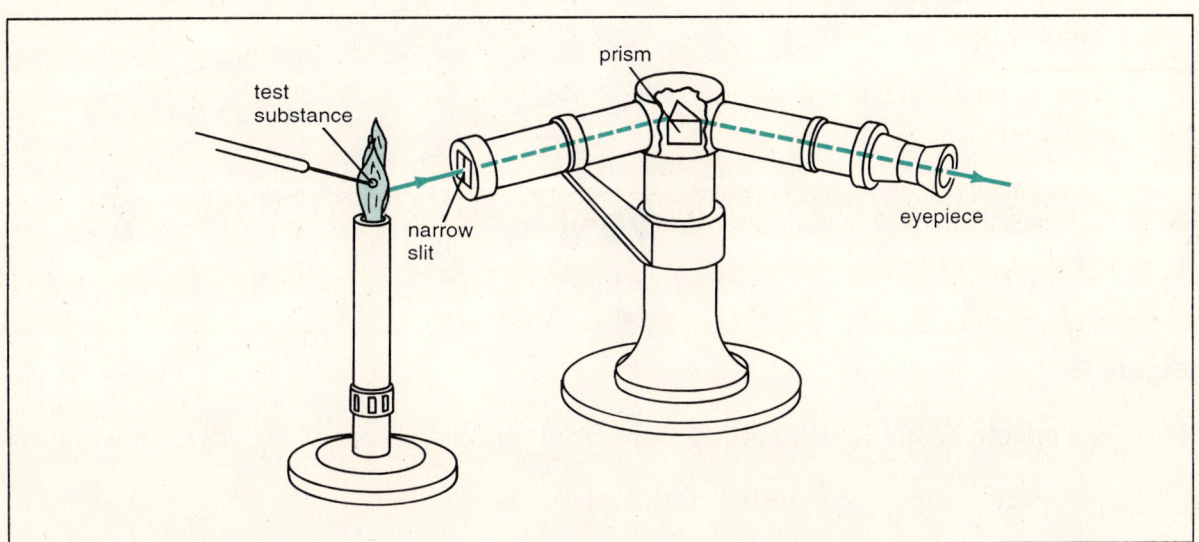

Figure B   *Spectroscope*

In a spectroscope, a prism breaks up the spectrums of individual substances.

1. The substance to be tested is placed in a flame. The flame is in line with the narrow slit of the spectroscope.

2. Light from the heated substance enters the slit.

3. The light passes through the prism.

4. The prism "breaks up" the light. A particular spectrum is formed.

5. The spectrum passes through the eyepiece into the eye of the viewer. The observer identified the spectrum.

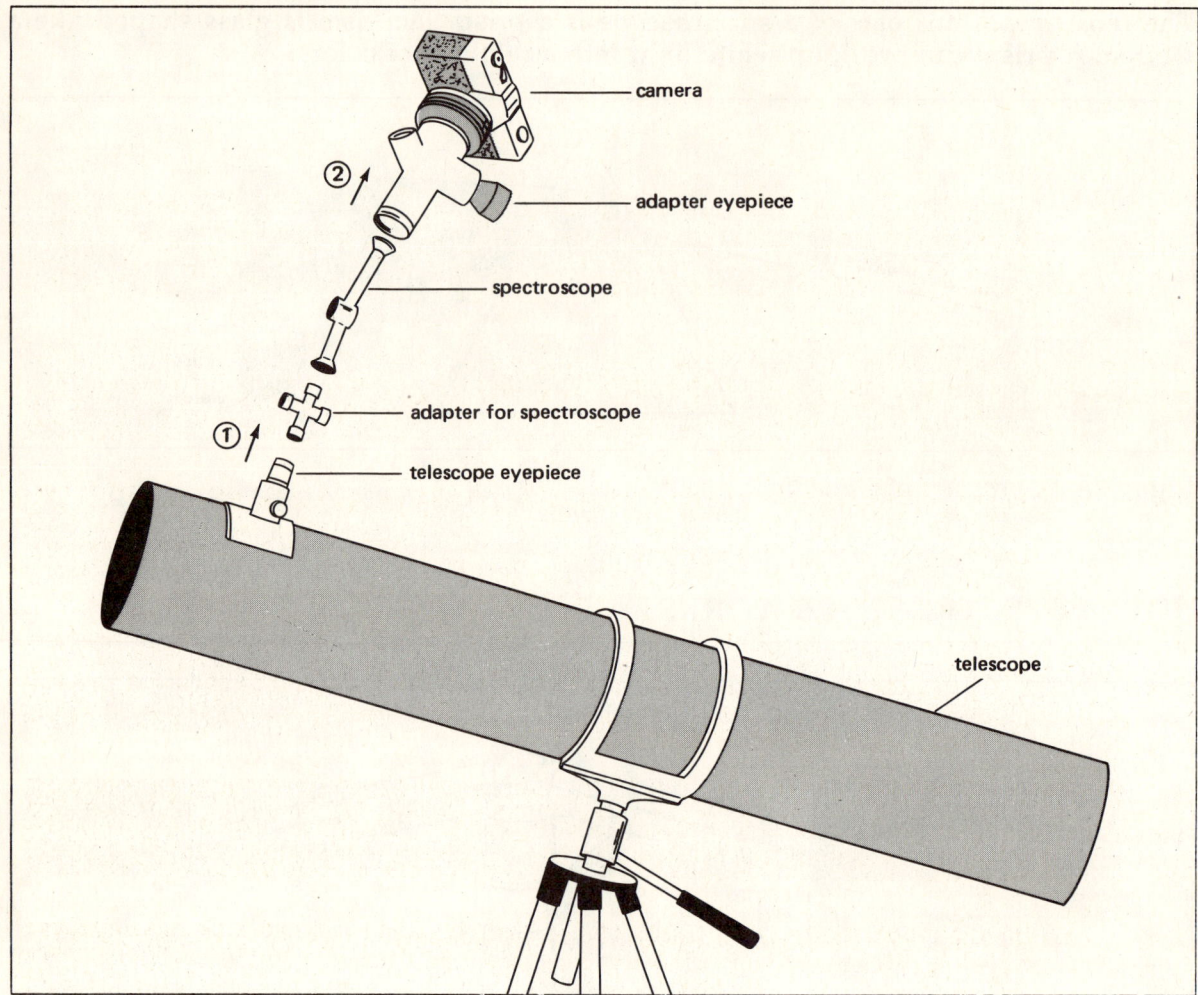

Figure C

How is a spectroscope used to study light from objects in space? Figure C shows how.

1. The spectroscope is connected to the telescope.

2. A camera is connected to the spectroscope.

3. The camera photographs the spectrum.

4. Astronomers study and identify the spectrum.

The spectroscope does more than identify the chemical make up of the sun and the stars. We can use the spectroscope to figure out:

- the makeup of the atmosphere of planets
- how fast a heavenly body moves
- in what direction a heavenly body moves
- how hot a star is
- if a star is rotating
- if a star has a magnetic field

SPECTRUMS OF ELEMENTS

Figure D shows the spectrums of 9 elements. The numbers stand for different wavelengths (colors).

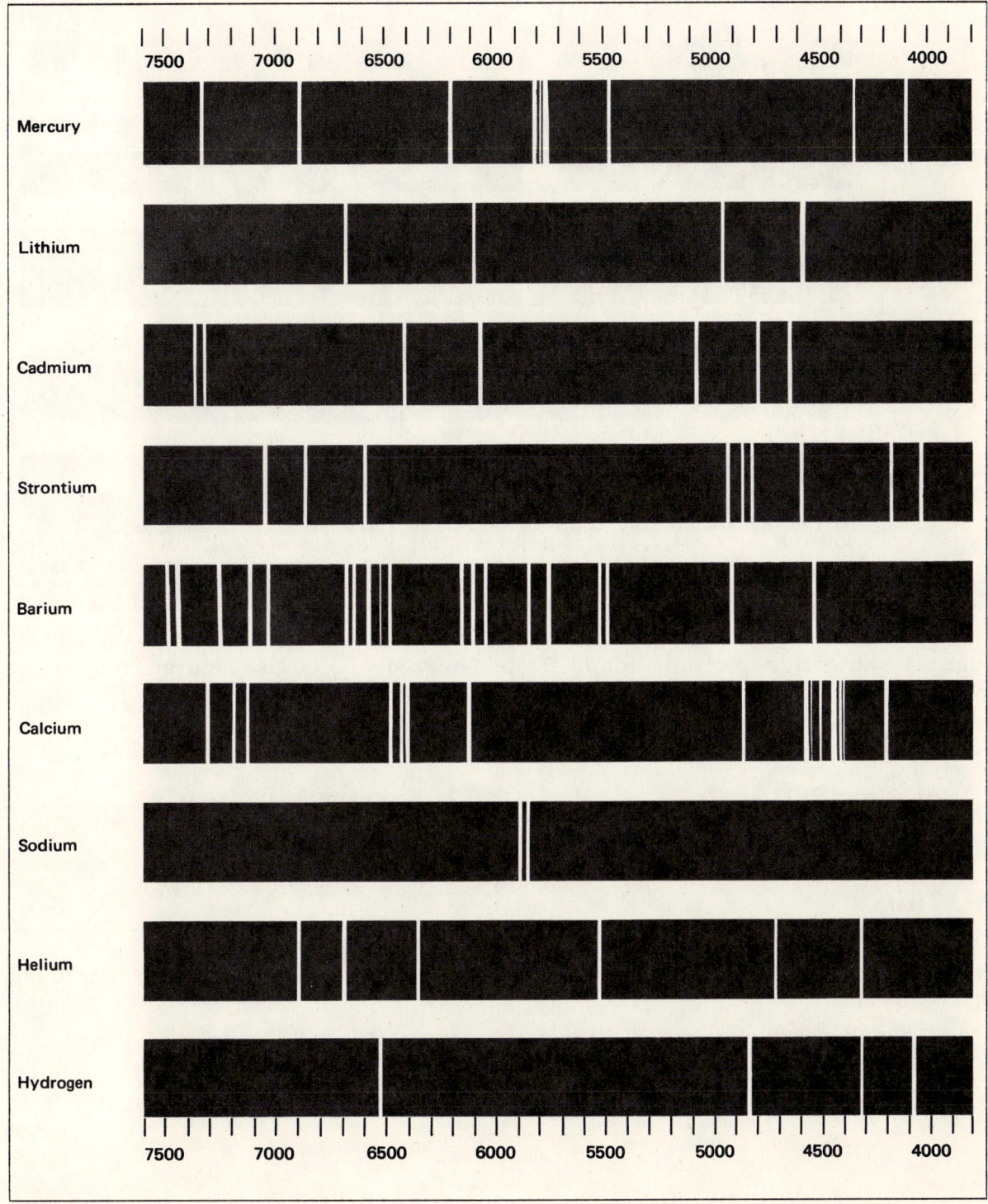

Figure D

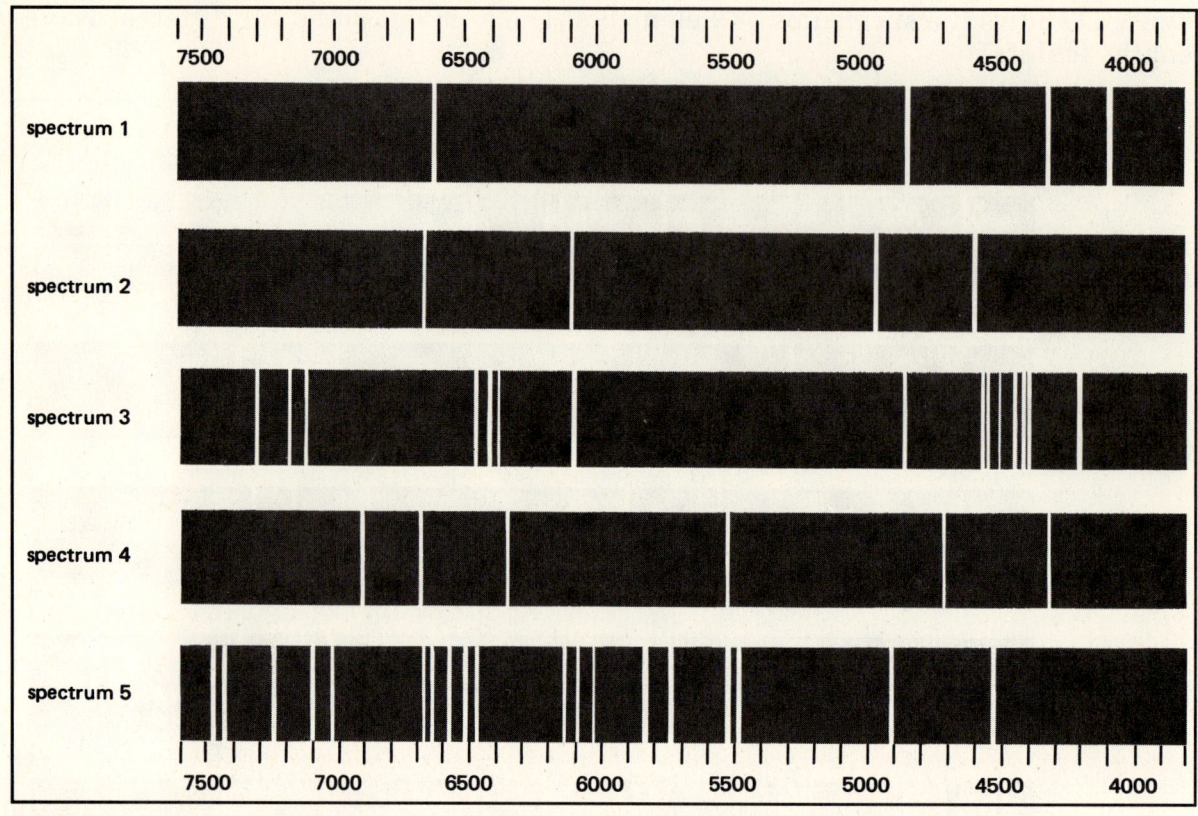

Figure E

Figure E shows five spectrums coming from a heavenly body. Use Figure D to find out which element is shown by each spectrum. Write your answers below.

1. Spectrum 1: _____   **4.** Spectrum 4: _____

2. Spectrum 2: _____   **5.** Spectrum 5: _____

3. Spectrum 3: _____

MATCHING

Match each term in Column A with its description in Column B. Write the correct letter in the space provided.

	Column A		Column B
_____	1. astronomy	a)	key part of a spectroscope
_____	2. optical telescope	b)	band of colors
_____	3. spectroscope	c)	analyzes light
_____	4. prism	d)	magnifies an image
_____	5. spectrum	e)	study of the heavens

18

How do astronomers measure distances?

4

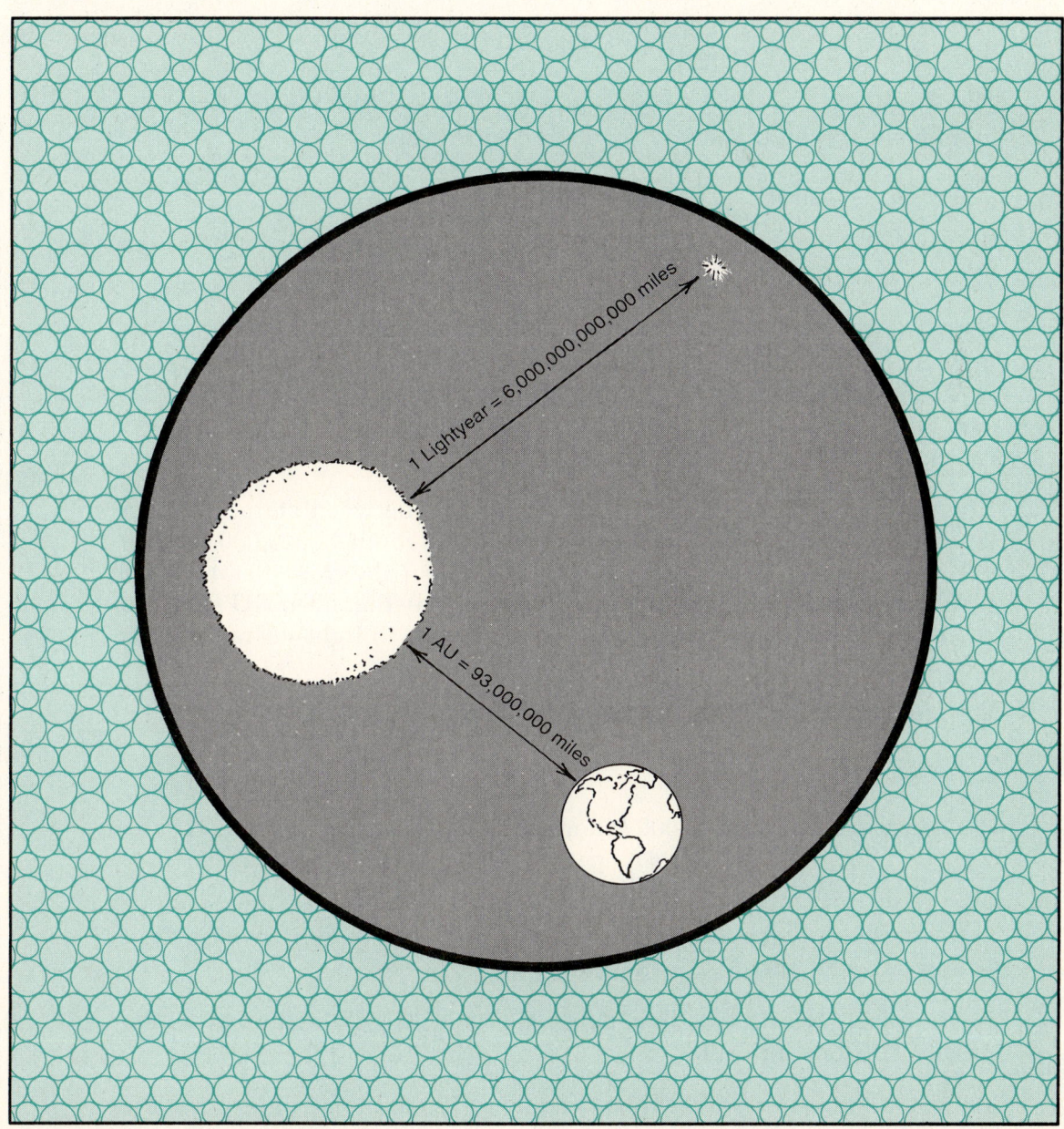

1 Lightyear = 6,000,000,000,000 miles

1 AU = 93,000,000 miles

astronomical [as-truh-NOM-ih-kul] **unit:**   distance between the Earth and Sun; 150,000,000 kilometers
light-year: the distance that light travels in one year

LESSON 4 | How do astronomers measure distances?

How far away from school do you live? A few miles, maybe? How thick is this book? A centimeter or so. You use different measurements all the time. The unit you use (centimeters, meters, kilometers, miles) depends upon what you are measuring.

The distances measured by astronomers are big. VERY BIG. Astronomers have special units they use to measure distances.

Our sun is far away — about 150 million kilometers away.

Think of it! You would need to fly around the earth more than 1800 times to go that distance.

Astronomers call the distance to the sun an **astronomical** [as-truh-NOM-ih-kul] **unit** (AU). So one AU equals about 150,000,000 kilometers. Jupiter is 778,300,000 kilometers away or a little more than 5 AU away from the sun. So Jupiter is about 5 times as far from the sun as Earth is. It is much easier to use AUs than kilometers.

An AU is very large. However, the distances between stars are even larger. Much larger. The closest star to the sun is about 42,000,000,000,000 kilometers away. That is 282,000 AU, and that is the closest star. Other stars are much farther. Some stars are so far away that even AU's are too small. The distances between stars are measured in light-years. What is a light-year?

A **light-year** is the distance that light travels in one year.

Let's see what this means.

• Light travels about 300,000 kilometers (186,000 miles) every second.

• There are 31,536,000 seconds in a year.

• If you multiply the seconds in a year by the speed of light, you find out how far light travels in one year.

How far is it? Nearly 10 trillion (10,000,000,000,000) kilometers (6 trillion miles). This one light-year.

10 trillion kilometers! Wow! That's equal to 125 million trips around the world.

HOW FAR AWAY ARE THE PLANETS

The table below shows how far away the planets are form the sun.

Planet	Astronomical Units	Kilometers
Mercury	0.4	58,000,000
Venus	0.7	108,000,000
Earth	1.0	150,000,000
Mars	1.5	230,000,000
Jupiter	5.2	778,000,000
Saturn	9.5	1,427,000,000
Uranus	19.2	2,870,000,000
Neptune	30.1	4,500,000,000
Pluto	39.4	5,900,000,000

To travel the distance between the sun and Pluto, you would have to circle the Earth more than 460,000 times!

HOW FAR AWAY ARE THE STARS

Figure A

The closest star to Earth (other than the sun) is 4.3 light-years away.

That's **423,000,000,000,000 kilometers** or **267,000,000,000,000 miles**.

Now here is something to think about. Most other stars are millions and hundreds of millions of light-years away! In fact, some stars in distance galaxies are believed to be about 16 million light years away.

That's **16,000,000,000,000,000,000,000 kilometers** or **9,600,000,000000,000,000,000 miles**.

FILL IN THE BLANK

Complete each statement using a term or terms from the list below. Write your answers in the spaces provided.

150,000,000	ten trillion	light
star	300,000	second
one year	light-year	stars
kilometers	sun	astronomical units
Earth		

1. The sun is a _____ .

2. The sun is _____ kilometers from Earth.

3. Distances between planets are measured in _____ .

4. One astronomical unit (AU) is the distance between _____ and

   the _____ .

5. All the other _____ are much farther away from Earth than the sun is.

6. We do not measure the distances between stars in _____ .

7. The distances between stars are measured in a unit called the

   _____ .

8. A light-year is the distance that _____ travels in _____ .

9. Light travels _____ kilometers per _____ .

10. One light-year is equal to about _____ kilometers.

REACHING OUT

People sometimes say that when we look at stars that are very far away that we are

"looking back in time." Why do people say this? _____

_____

_____

_____

What is parallax?

parallax [PAR-uh-laks]:   shift of position an object seems to have when it is seen from two
    different points

LESSON 5 | What is parallax?

Any object seems to shift position when it is viewed from two different points. We call this apparent shift in position **parallax** [PAR-uh-laks]. You can see parallax while sitting at your desk. Do this:

1. Hold one finger a short distance in front of your face.

2. Close your right eye.

3. Now open your right eye and close your left eye.

4. Repeat this several times.

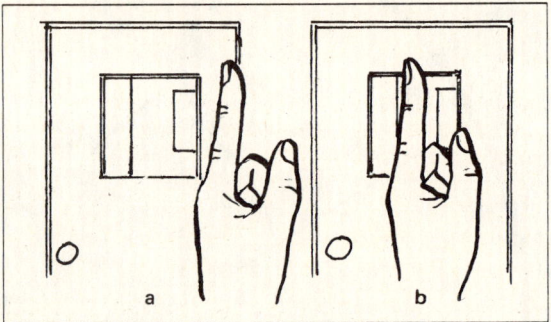

Your finger did not move. But it seemed to. It seemed to move back and forth compared to the background. It is this apparent shift that we call parallax.

Parallax lets us measure the distances to many stars. It even helps us measure the size of the sun, moon, and planets.

Some stars are so far away that scientists cannot use parallax to figure out how far away they are. Scientists use other methods to try to determine how far away these stars are.

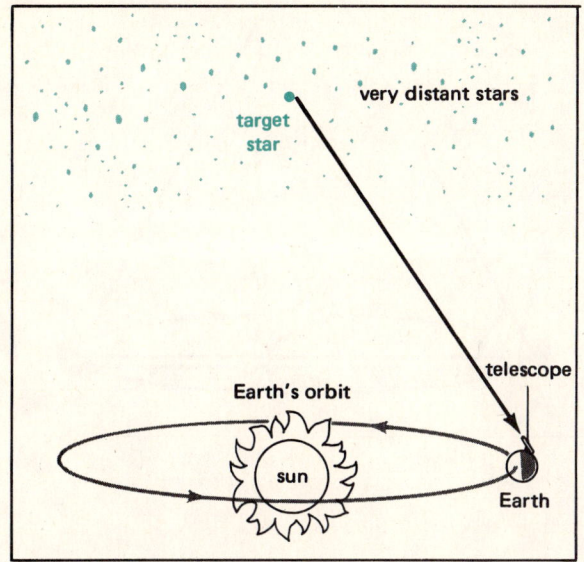

Figure A

Step 1 A nearby "target" star is chosen. Distance stars are in the background. They are photographed together.

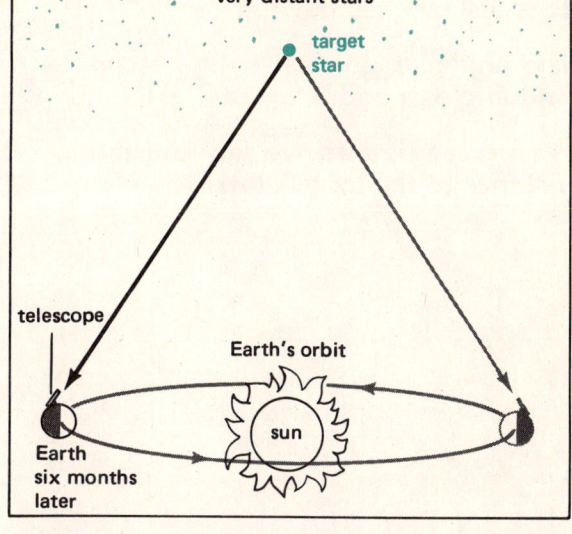

Figure B

Step 2 A second photograph is made six months later. The earth is then exactly at the opposite end of its path around the sun.

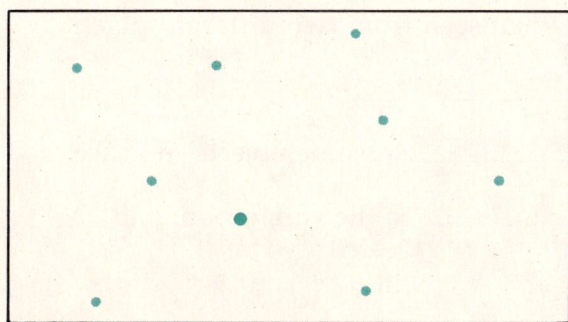

Figure C *The first photo*

Figure D *The photo taken six months later*

Compare the photos. Notice that the target star is not in the same spot. It seems to have shifted compared to the reference stars. Astronomers measure the angle the target star seems to have shifted. This angle is called the angle of greatest shift.

The final step is simple math. A triangle is set up as in Figure E.

The base is the distance between the earth's position six months apart. This distance is known.

The angle of greatest shift lets us find angles a and b.

With these figures, we can find the distance to the target star.

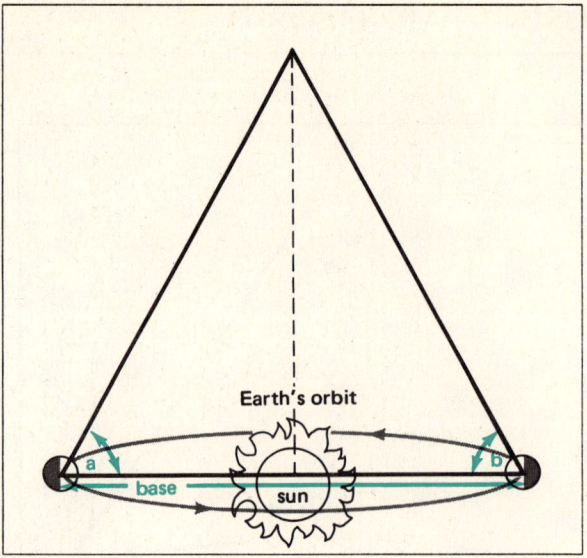

Figure E

FILL IN THE BLANK

Complete each statement using a term or terms from the list below. Write your answers in the spaces provided. Some words may be used more than once.

distances   halfway   shift position   kilometers
two   parallax   light-years   six months

1. Every object seems to _____ when seen from two different places.

2. This apparent shift in position is called_____ .

3. Parallax allows us to measure the _____ to some objects in space.

4. Parallax can be used to measure _____ to the sun, moon, and

   planets.

5. To measure the distance to a star, at least _____ observations are needed.

6. For the best results, the second observation is made exactly _____

   after the first.

7. In six months the earth has traveled _____ through its path around the sun.

8. The distances between stars is measured in _____ , not in

   _____ .

26

How does a rocket move? 6

action: a force
reaction: an opposing force that balances an action

LESSON 6 | How does a rocket move?

Did you ever blow up a balloon and let go suddenly? What happened? It flew through the air. It zigzagged a bit. But generally, it flew in the direction <u>opposite</u> to the mouthpiece.

The balloon acted like a small rocket. It moved forward as the air was escaping from the mouthpiece.

Huge rockets have lifted astronauts into space. Smaller rockets have placed satellites into orbit around the earth. Large or small, all rockets work on the same idea—even your balloon "rocket."

What is this idea?

You have heard of Isaac Newton. He explained gravity and inertia. Newton also helped explain how a rocket moves. It is explained in Newton's *Third Law of Motion*. This law says that every time there is a force acting upon an object in one direction there is an equally strong force acting in the opposite direction.

• The first force is called the **action**.

• The opposite force is called the **reaction**.

The scientific way to state Newton's *Third Law of Motion* is:

For every action, there is an equal reaction in the opposite direction.

In a rocket, the action pushes downward. This force comes from fuel burning in the rocket's engines. You have probably seen films of flames shooting downward during a blastoff. As the hot gases move downward, the rocket moves upward into the sky . . . And away it goes!

A balloon can move like a rocket. Figures A and B show two blown-up balloons.

• The mouthpiece of the balloon in Figure A is closed.

• The mouthpiece of the balloon in Figure B has just been opened.

Look at the figures.

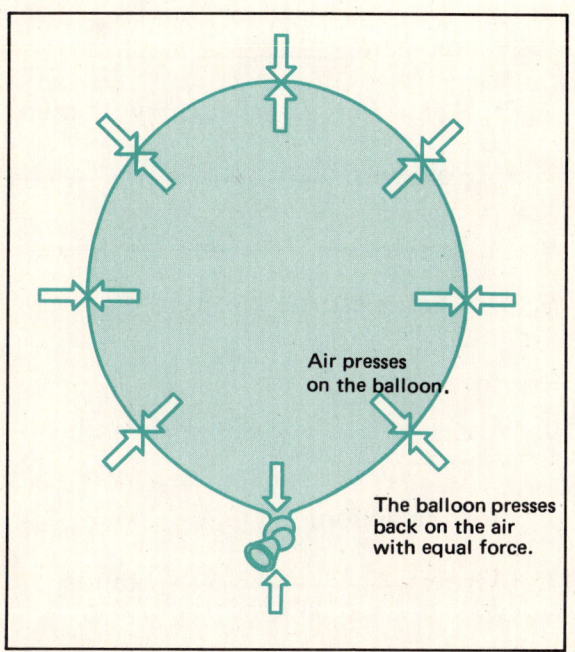

Air presses on the balloon.

The balloon presses back on the air with equal force.

Figure A

Answer these questions about the balloon in Figure A.

1. The forces _____
   are, are not

   balanced.

2. The balloon _____
   will, will not

   move forward.

3. Does a closed blown-up balloon

   move like a rocket? _____

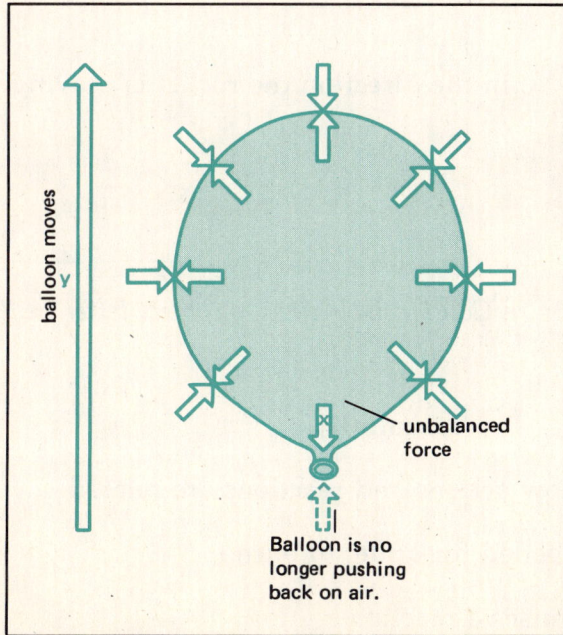

balloon moves

y

unbalanced force

Balloon is no longer pushing back on air.

Figure B

Answer these questions about the balloon in Figure B.

4. The forces are _____
   still, no longer

   balanced.

5. Some air is escaping from

   _____ .
   x, y

6. As the air escapes, it causes the balloon to move in the direction of

   _____ .
   x y

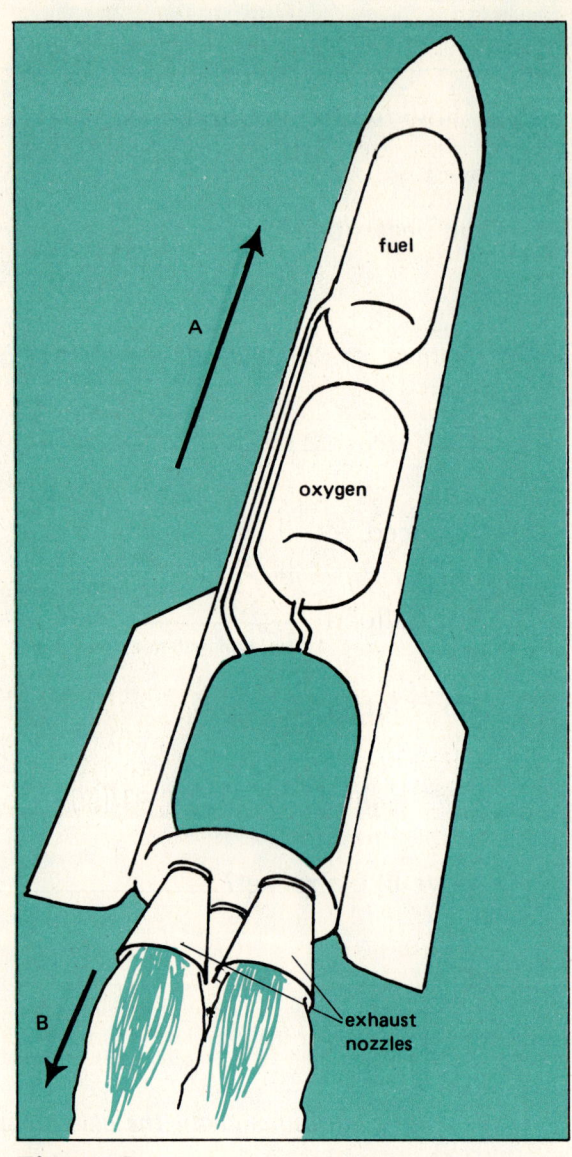

Figure C

Figure C shows a rocket. Study Figure C. Answer the questions.

7. A rocket carries fuel. What else does a rocket carry? _____

Oxygen helps the fuel to burn.

8. a) Does an airplane carry its own oxygen? _____

   b) Why does a rocket carry its own oxygen? _____

   _____

9. Hot gases escape through the _____ .

10. Arrow————————— stands
    A, B

    for the action.

11. Arrow————————— stands
    A, B

    for the reaction.

12. Arrow _____ points
    A, B

    in the direction the rocket is moving.

MATCHING

Match each term in Column A with its description in Column B. Write the correct letter in the space provided.

Column A	Column B
_____ 1. an action	a) how actions and reactions are related
_____ 2. opposite	b) needed for a fuel to burn
_____ 3. fuel	c) causes a reaction
_____ 4. oxygen	d) wrote the *Third Law of Motion*
_____ 5. Isaac Newton	e) burns

THE SATURN V

The Saturn V rocket was America's most powerful rocket. This rocket took astronauts to the moon.

Here are some interesting facts about the Saturn V:

- The Saturn V stands 111 meters (364 feet) tall. This is 18 meters (59 feet) taller than the Statue of Liberty.

- At lift-off, it uses 13.6 metric tons (15 tons) of fuel every second. This is enough fuel to run a family car for nearly 5 years.

- Its lift-off mass is 2,721,5543 kilograms (about 6,000,000 pounds). This is equal to the mass of 20 loaded airliners—or 1,818 medium-sized cars.

Figure D

EXPERIENCES WITH ACTIONS AND REACTIONS

Look at Figures E through H. Each figure shows an action and a reaction.

Identify the action and reaction in each picture. Answer by letter.

Figure E

1. Action ——————

   Reaction ——————

Figure F

2. Action ——————

   Reaction ——————

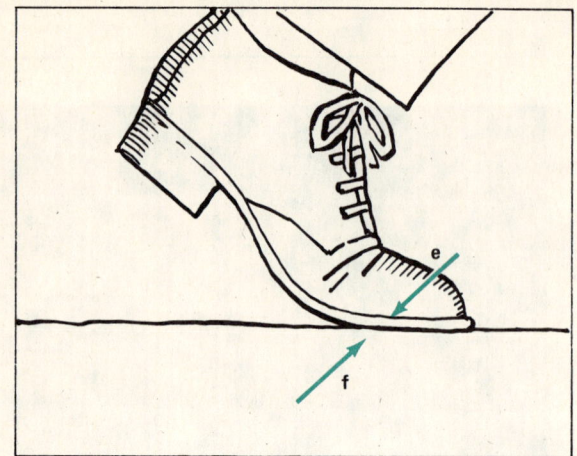

Figure G

3. Action _____

   Reaction _____

Figure H

4. Action _____

   Reaction _____

FILL IN THE BLANK

Complete each statement using a term or terms from the list below. Write your answers in the spaces provided.

Saturn V	left	Isaac Newton
fuel	down	opposite
action	reaction	oxygen

1. The scientist who stated the *Third Law of Motion* was _____ .

2. Newton's *Third Law of Motion* states that every _____ has an equal

   _____ .

3. Actions and reactions are _____ in direction.

4. If the direction of an action is up, then the direction of a reaction is

   _____ .

5. If the direction of an action is to the right, then the direction of a reaction is to the

   _____ .

6. Rockets sent into space carry _____ and _____ .

7. America's most powerful rocket was the _____ .

What are satellites and space probes?

satellite [SAT-uh-lite]:   an object that revolves around another object
space probe: a machine that is sent from Earth to study other objects in space

LESSON 7 | What are satellites and space probes?

The moon is a satellite of the earth. A **satellite** [SAT-uh-lite] is something that orbits another object in space.

On October 4, 1957, the Soviet Union launched Sputnik into orbit around the earth. Sputnik became the earth's first artificial satellite.

Since Sputnik, hundreds of satellites have been launched. Satellites perform all sorts of functions. There are four basic types of satellites.

EARTH SENSING SATELLITES These satellites have cameras or some other kind of sensors pointed down at the earth. As the satellite flies over different places, the sensors on the satellite study these places. Satellites are very helpful in the study of isolated places that are hard for people to get to, such as the tops of mountains. Earth sensing satellites also are used by the military of some countries to study what is going on in other countries.

SPACE SENSING SATELLITES We need the earth's atmosphere to survive, but the atmosphere often is in the way when we try to study things in space. Satellites are often put in orbit above the earth's atmosphere. These satellites have a clear view of what scientists want to study in space.

COMMUNICATION SATELLITES Radio waves cannot travel through the ground, and the curvature of the earth gets in the way of radio signals that are sent far across the planet. Instead, radio signals are sent to satellites in space. The satellites, in turn, send the signal to another place on the earth. In fact, sometimes a satellite sends a message on to another satellite which then sends it to the ground. Messages can be sent all the way around the world this way.

NAVIGATION SATELLITES Ships, planes, and even cars can pinpoint their location on the earth by "listening" to the signals sent by several navigation satellites.

Figure A *The TIROS weather satellite helps weathermen make their forecasts.*

Figure B *The Solar Maximum satellite studies the sun from space.*

Figure C *The Intelsat satellite relays telephone calls and television programs.*

Figure D *The Navstar satellite helps ships, aircraft and land vehicles navigate.*

Figure E *Voyager*

In studying planets and other objects in the solar system, sometimes there is no substitute for "being there." However, it would be very expensive, and very dangerous, to send people to other planets. Instead, scientists send robots similar to satellites toward these objects. These robots are called space probes.

Space probes come in all shapes and sizes and can perform various functions. Most space probes have cameras of some type to take pictures of the objects they are studying. Because space probes are much closer to the objects they are studying, they can take much better pictures than we can from Earth. *Voyager 1* and *Voyager 2* are two space probes that flew by Jupiter, Saturn, Uranus, and Neptune.

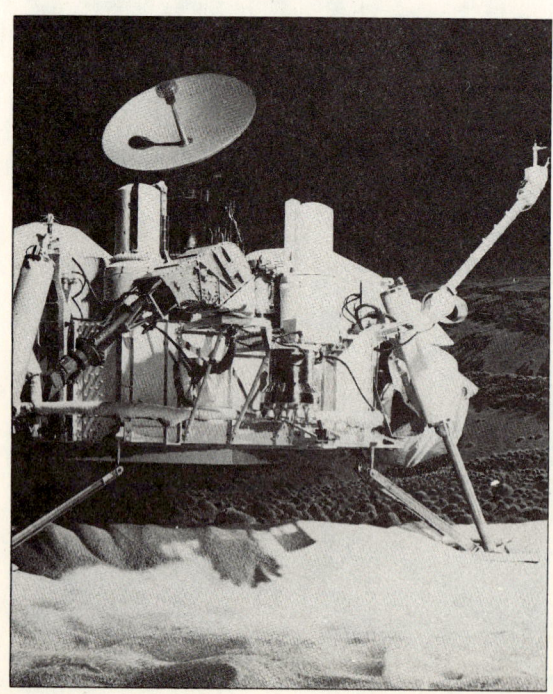

Figure F *Viking*

Some space probes are designed to land on other planets. These probes can then study the surface of the planet. *Viking 1* and *Viking 2* were two probes that landed on Mars in 1976.

TRUE OR FALSE

In the space provided, write "true" if the sentence is true. Write "false" if the sentence is false.

_____   1. Sputnik was the earth's first satellite.

_____   2. Sputnik was the earth's first artificial satellite.

_____   3. The earth has one natural satellite.

_____   4. The earth has no natural satellites.

_____   5. Satellites can be used to study the earth.

_____   6. Satellites can be used to study space.

_____   7. Space probes carry people to other planets.

_____   8. Space probes study objects in space.

_____   9. Space probes cannot land on planets.

_____   10. *Voyager 1* and *Voyager 2* studied Mars.

MATCHING

Match each term in Column A with its description in Column B. Write the correct letter in the space provided.

Column A

_____   1. navigation satellites

_____   2. earth sensing satellites

_____   3. space sensing satellites

_____   4. communication satellites

_____   5. space probes

Column B

a) used to study other objects in space from earth orbit

b) weather satellites

c) *Voyager 1* and *Voyager 2*

d) relay telephone calls and television programs

e) help ships, planes, and cars find their way

WORD SEARCH

The list on the left contains words that you have used in this Lesson. Find and circle each word where it appears in the box. The spellings may go in any direction: up, down, left, right, or diagonally.

SATELLITE
NAVIGATION
ROCKET
VOYAGER
VIKING
COMMUNICATION
NEWTON
EARTH
SPACE
MARS

```
D  C  U  T  S  P  A  C  E  E  N  E
E  O  I  T  R  S  S  A  B  T  F  I
R  M  I  R  E  G  A  Y  O  V  T  Y
T  M  H  O  E  V  T  O  B  I  E  R
R  U  O  C  R  J  E  P  N  K  I  T
E  N  I  K  W  N  L  R  E  I  S  I
F  I  G  E  F  O  L  F  W  N  Y  G
I  C  H  T  B  Z  I  Q  T  G  D  O
N  A  V  I  G  A  T  I  O  N  Z  L
E  T  A  L  S  O  E  D  N  E  L  A
J  I  K  E  A  R  T  H  V  O  J  K
I  O  M  X  N  M  A  R  E  E  T  H
M  N  J  U  P  T  Q  M  L  M  S  T
```

REACHING OUT

Why is it cheaper to send space probes to other planets instead of sending people?

_____

_____

_____

_____

What is a space shuttle? 8

space shuttle: reusable space vehicle

LESSON 8 | What is a space shuttle?

Imagine that your family owned a car that could be used JUST ONCE. After only one trip — long or short, it had to be junked. Sounds ridiculous? It certainly does! But this is precisely how the space program operated until April 12, 1981. On that date, Columbia, America's first Space Shuttle was launched. It went into orbit — and then returned to earth.

A **Space Shuttle** is a reusable space vehicle. Until the Shuttle, no part of a space launch (that blasted off) was reused. Some parts fell into the ocean. Others burned up while returning to Earth. Even the capsules that carried astronauts were not reused.

This approach to space exploration was too expensive. Scientists knew this. They wanted a cheaper way to send things into space, so they developed the Space Shuttle.

The Space Shuttle is designed to be used over and over again. Only one part — its main fuel tank must be replaced.

A Space Shuttle system has three main parts:

• the Shuttle orbiter itself, with its three main engines

• two solid rocket boosters (for extra thrust)

• external tank (a large fuel tank)

1. At blastoff, all parts are connected. The main engines and the boosters both burn with a deafening roar. The Shuttle lifts off and heads towards space.

2. After a few minutes, the boosters have used up their fuel. They separate and parachute back to earth. They are recovered and re-used. The main fuel tank is still attached and continues to feed the main engines.

3. When the Shuttle reaches its proper speed and position, the main fuel tank breaks away. It burns up as it plunges back through the atmosphere. This is the only part that is not reused.

4. The Shuttle is now in orbit around the Earth. It may continue in orbit for several days. While in orbit, the crew carries out their mission.

5. Its mission completed, the Shuttle returns to earth. Since it has no fuel, it glides back to earth.

6. The Shuttle lands on wheels, like an airplane. It is then made ready to be reused.

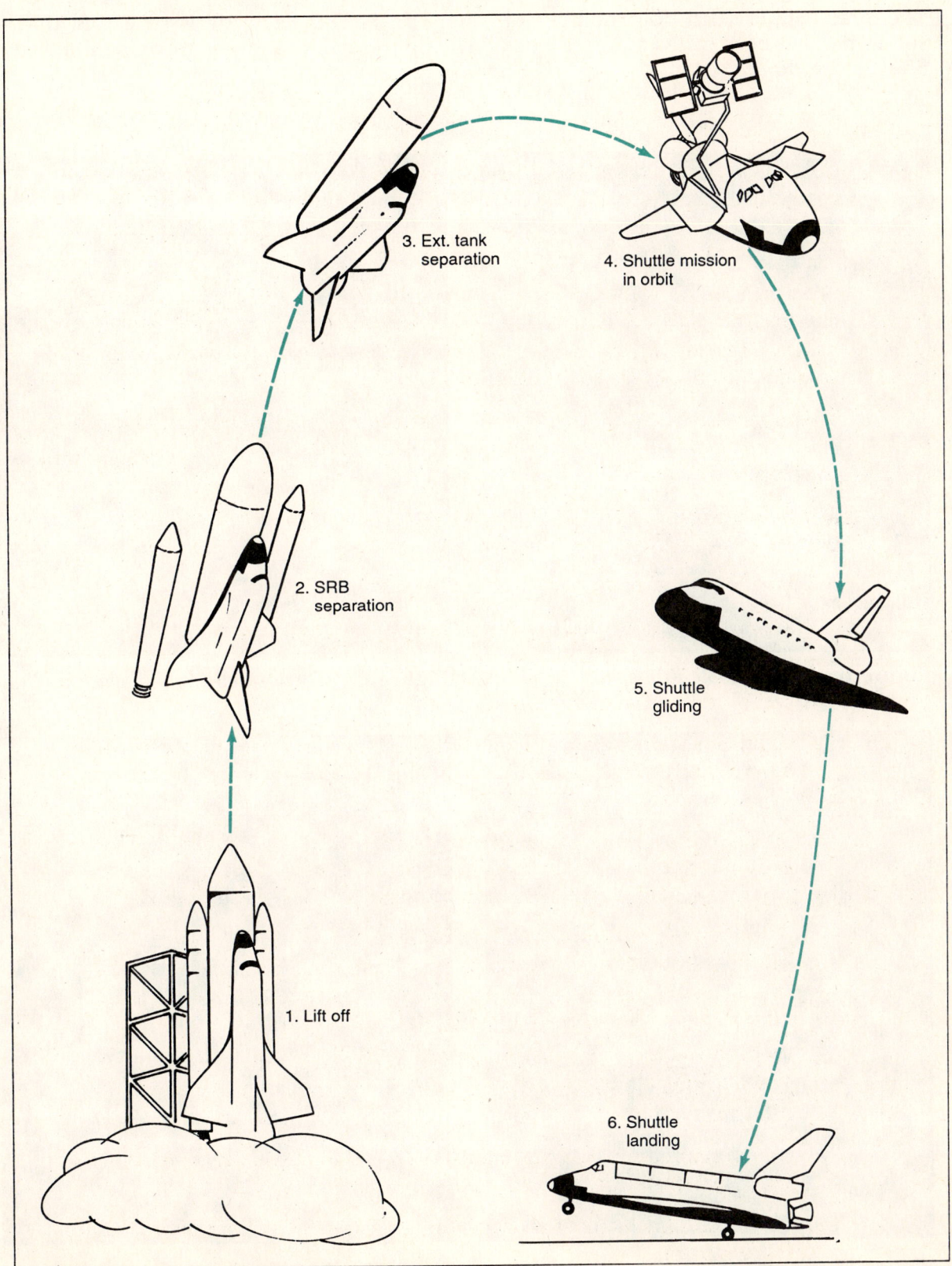

3. Ext. tank
separation

4. Shuttle mission
in orbit

2. SRB
separation

5. Shuttle
gliding

1. Lift off

6. Shuttle
landing

Figure A

USES OF THE SPACE SHUTTLE

The Space Shuttle can do a number of things. In fact, the Shuttle is so useful that it sometimes has been called a "space truck." The figures below show some of the things the Shuttle can do.

Figure B *Carry people into space*

Figure C *Carry satellites and space probes*

Figure D *Return objects from space to Earth*

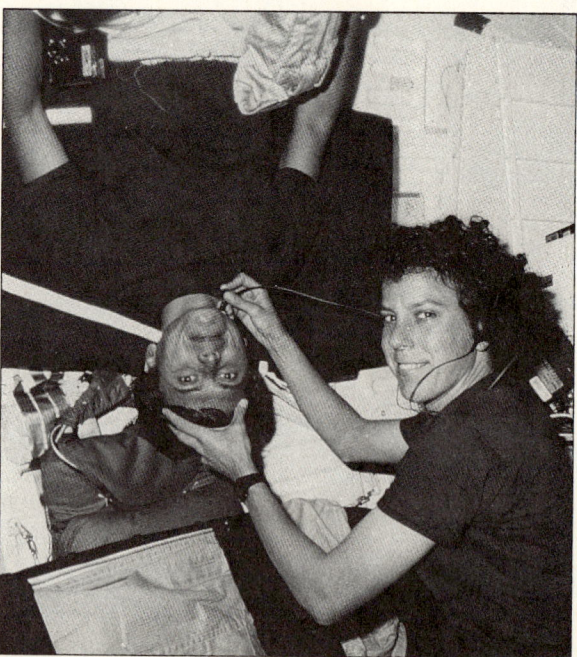

Figure E *Perform experiments in zero gravity*

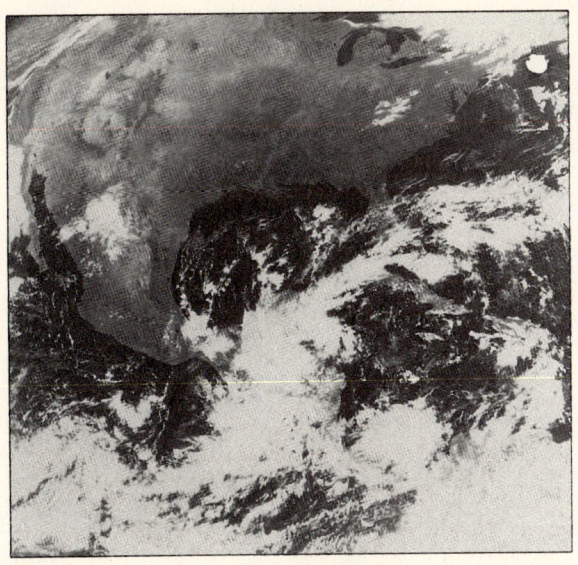

Figure F *Study Earth from space*

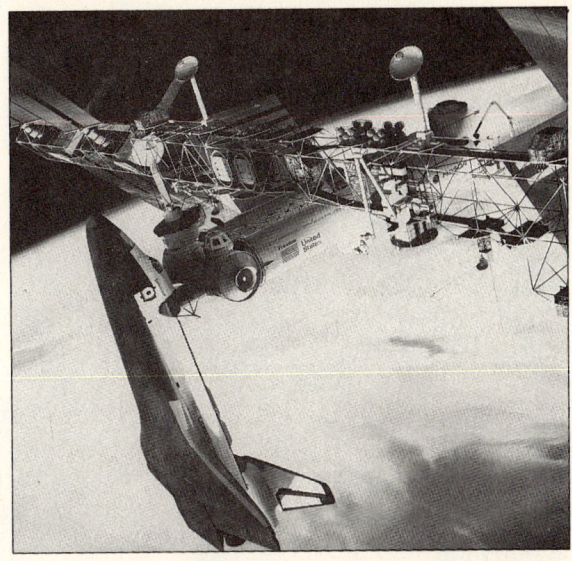

Figure G *Build and supply a space station*

TRUE OR FALSE

In the space provided, write "true" if the sentence is true. Write "false" if the sentence is false.

_____ **1.** The Shuttle has two solid rocket boosters.

_____ **2.** The external tank is carried into space.

_____ **3.** The external tank is not reusable.

_____ **4.** The Shuttle only carries people into space.

_____ **5.** The Shuttle has a large cargo bay to carry things into space.

_____ **6.** The Shuttle lands on water.

_____ **7.** The Shuttle lands like an airplane.

_____ **8.** The Shuttle takes off like an airplane.

_____ **9.** The Shuttle takes off like a rocket.

_____ **10.** The Shuttle can bring satellites back to Earth.

FILL IN THE BLANK

Complete each statement using a term or terms from the list below. Write your answers in the spaces provided. Some words may be used more than once.

launch   external tank   solid rocket boosters
orbits   shuttle orbiter   joined
Space Shuttle   repair   glides
wheels   is not

1. The _____ is the first reusable spacecraft.

2. The main parts of a Shuttle system are the _____ , two

    _____ and an _____ .

3. Extra upward thrust is supplied by the _____ .

4. At lift-off, all the parts of the Shuttle system are _____ .

5. The first parts of the Shuttle system to separate, are the _____ .

6. The external tank _____ reused.

7. The shuttle _____ Earth.

8. Not only can the Shuttle be used to _____ satellites, it can be used to

    _____ them.

9. When its mission is completed, the Shuttle _____ back to earth.

10. The Shuttle lands on _____ like a regular airplane.

REACHING OUT

Will the Shuttle last forever? Why or why not? _____

_____

_____

How do humans survive in space?

9

dehydrated [dee-HY-drayt-ed]:   an item in which water has been removed
environment [in-VY-run-munt]:   the surroundings that living things live in

LESSON 9 | How do humans survive in space?

Everything that surrounds an organism is called its **environment.** Air and water are parts of the environment. So are the temperature, air pressure, and food.

Our environment is well suited for life. We have air to breathe, food to eat, and water to drink. The air pressure is just right. In most places the temperature is never too hot or too cold. The atmosphere blocks out harmful radiation. In short, we live in a "friendly" environment.

The environment in space, however, is not friendly to humans. It presents many problems. You could not live in space the same way that you live on earth. There is no air to breathe. There is also no air pressure. The temperature is either much too hot or much too cold. No food grows in space. And there is nothing to block out harmful radiation.

There are other problems too. Living things produce wastes. The wastes must be eliminated. On earth, we have no problem eliminating our wastes. Every time we breathe out we release carbon dioxide into the air. Heat and moisture from our skin goes into the air, too. We use water to flush away the liquid and solid wastes we produce.

In space, getting rid of wastes is not so easy. In fact, just keeping clean is a problem.

On earth, gravity holds you to the ground. In a moving spacecraft, there is no gravity. Actually, gravity from outer space does pull upon the spacecraft. But the movement of the spacecraft cancels it out. The result is "zero" gravity. In zero gravity a person seems to weigh nothing. Just imagine. You would float around the spacecraft if you didn't hold onto something!

Because of all these problems of living in space, astronauts must bring along their own environment! It must be like the environment found on earth. Special clothing and instruments have been designed so that the traveler in space has everything that is needed to stay alive.

LIVING IN A SPACECRAFT

Look at the figures. Answer the questions.

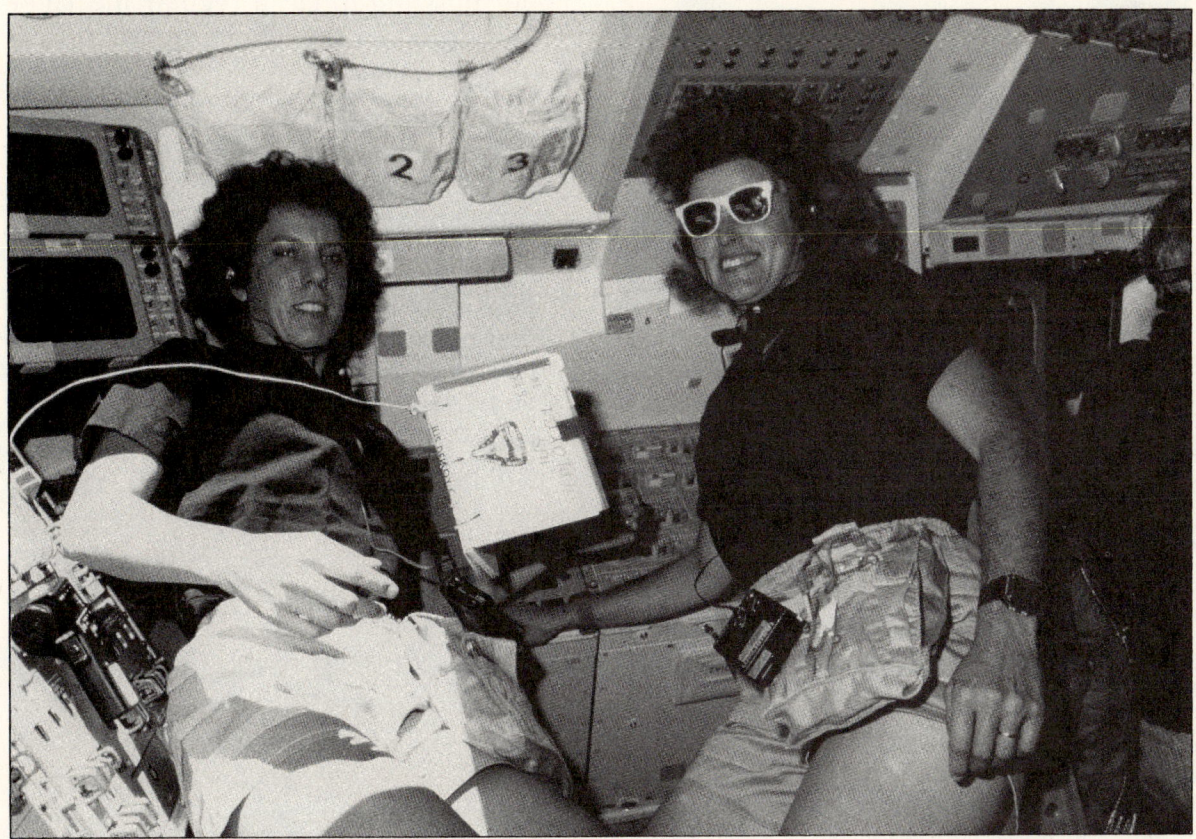

Figure A *Inside a spacecraft in flight: like a little part of the earth—far from earth.*

Outside the spacecraft the temperature is extremely cold.

1. The temperature inside the spacecraft _____ extremely cold.

is, is not

Outside the spacecraft, there is no air pressure.

2. People _____ live where there is no air pressure.

can, cannot

3. The air inside the spacecraft is _____ .

cold, pressurized

4. The pressure inside the cabin is like the air pressure _____ .

on Earth, in space

The spacecraft carries tanks of oxygen.

5. We _____ live without oxygen.

can, cannot

EATING IN SPACE

Figure B

Everything in space is weightless. It is not possible to eat a regular meal like you do on earth. The food would float around inside the cabin. An astronaut would have to chase after the meal.

Early astronauts ate soft foods from tubes that looked like toothpaste tubes. The astronauts would squeeze the food right into their mouths.

The Space Shuttle has a galley where the crew can prepare meals. This galley even has an oven to heat up premade foods. Some food is dehydrated [dee-HY-drat-ed] so the shuttle astronauts must add water to it.

OUTSIDE THE SPACECRAFT

Figure C

An astronaut may not spend all the time in the spacecraft. Some of the time may be spent taking "space walks" in a pressurized space suit.

The space suit has air, food and water for the astronaut.

A "rocket" backpack allows astronauts to fly in space all by themselves.

1. Is there pressure outside the

   spacesuit? _____

2. Is there pressure inside the

   spacesuit? _____

WEIGHTLESSNESS IN SPACE

Figure D

Figure E

Very little can be done about weightlessness. Astronauts prepare themselves for this funny feeling. Airplanes can be piloted to mimic zero gravity. Astronauts also practice missions underwater. In this way an astronaut learns what to expect.

1. Do the astronauts feel the pull of gravity in a moving spacecraft? _____

2. How much do the astronauts seem to weigh there? _____

3. How do astronauts prepare for the feeling of weightlessness? _____

_____

4. How is being in water like being in space? _____

49

FILL IN THE BLANK

Complete each statement using a term or terms from the list below. Write your answers in the spaces provided.

temperature   airplanes   oxygen
spacecraft   earth   under water

1. A _____ must supply everything an astronaut needs.

2. The _____ in a spacecraft is kept at a comfortable level.

3. The pressure in a spacecraft is like the pressure on the _____ .

4. Living things need _____ to survive.

5. Astronauts train for weightlessness on _____ and _____ .

MATCHING

Match each term in Column A with its description in Column B. Write the correct letter in the space provided.

Column A

_____ 1. carbon dioxide

_____ 2. shields

_____ 3. airplane

_____ 4. space suit

_____ 5. oxygen

Column B

a) copies zero gravity

b) needed for life

c) carries everything the astronaut needs

d) block radiation

e) waste gas

REACHING OUT

Spacesuits are white. There is a good reason for this. What is this reason?

_____

_____

_____

What are the earth's motions?

revolution [reh-vuh-LOO-shun]:   the traveling of an object around another object
rotation [roh-TAY-shun]:   the spinning of an object on its axis

LESSON 10 | What are the earth's motions?

Find a quiet place where you can be alone for a few minutes. It can be anywhere—in your room, your yard, a park, or vacant lot or field. Just as long as you can look around and observe what's happening.

What is happening? If your answer is "nothing," think again. In the minute or so that you have been looking around, the spot you are standing on has moved. It has traveled a distance of about 17 kilometers (10 miles)! In 24 hours, that same spot will have traveled a circular distance of more than 25,000 kilometers (15,000 miles)!

And that's not all. While you are looking around, you are traveling through space. You are moving at a speed of about 30 kilometers (18 miles) per second!

How can this be? How can you be moving and not feel it? Or see it? The reason you can't sense the motion is because everything around you is moving too. Your home, the trees, the air and clouds—everything is moving at the same speed.

Actually, the entire earth is moving. In fact, there are two different motions of the earth. Both are happening at the same time.

First, the earth is "spinning like a top." It is turning, or rotating, on its axis. This motion is called **rotation** [roh-TAY-shun]. It takes the earth 24 hours to complete one rotation. This time period is called a day.

Second, the earth is moving through space. It is traveling, or revolving, around the sun. This motion is called **revolution** [reh-vuh-LOO-shun]. The earth completes one revolution in 365 1/4 days. This time period is called a year.

THE EARTH'S ROTATION

You cannot feel it, but the earth is spinning on its axis. It rotates from west to east. You may think, "So what? If I cannot feel it spinning, what difference does it make?"

Let's take a quick look at the "difference" rotation makes.

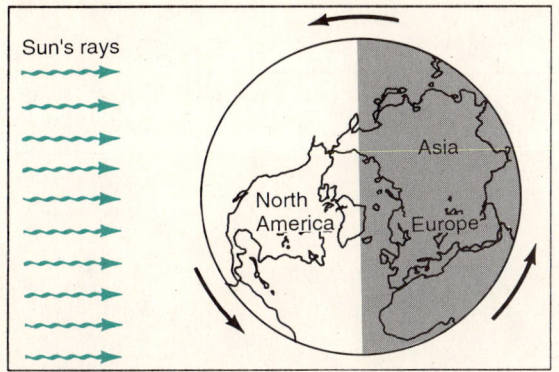 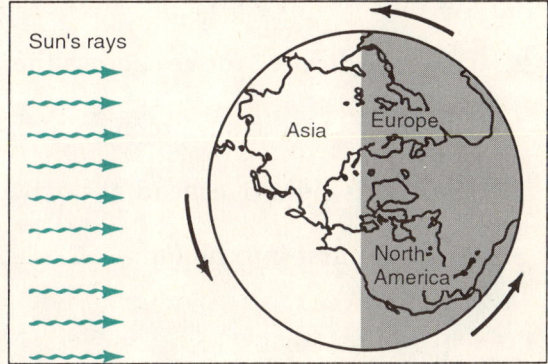

Figure A   **Figure B**

The Sun's rays can only shine on one side of the Earth at a time. It is daytime in the half of the Earth that gets the light and nighttime in the half of the Earth that does not get the light. As the Earth rotates the part of the Earth that the sun shines on **changes**. Every part of the Earth has daytime, then night time, then daytime again.

THE EARTH'S REVOLUTION

In one year, the earth travels about 940,000,000 kilometers! It *revolves* around the sun. You can't feel this motion either. But there are ways to tell the earth revolves. Look at Figure C.

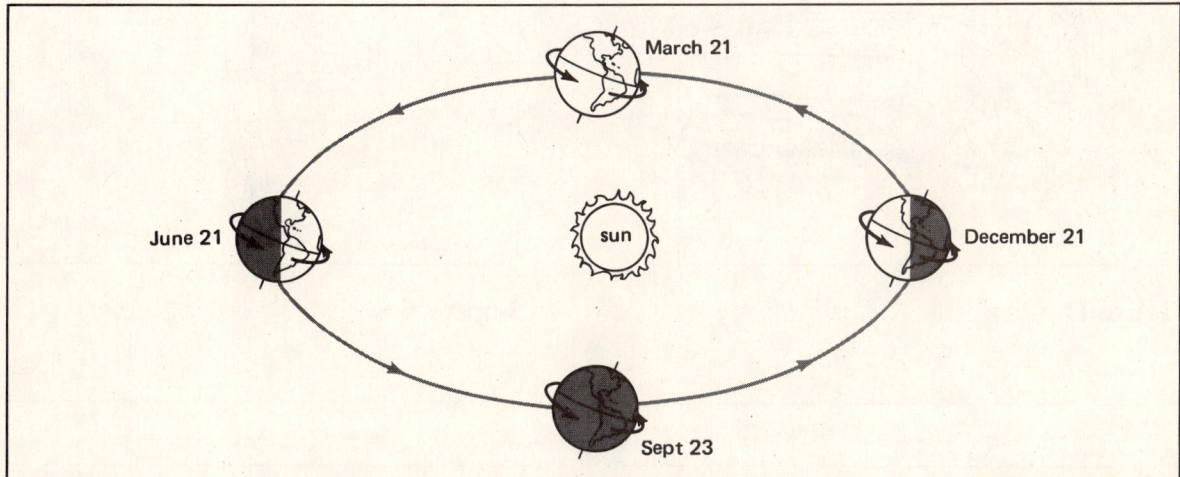

Figure C

The drawing shows the earth at different points in its trip around the sun. Notice the dates. At each of these dates, we start a different season. The earth's revolution (along with the tilt of its axis) causes the seasons.

ROTATION OR REVOLUTION?

Each statement describes something caused by one of the earth's motions. Beside each statement, write the word "rotation" or "revolution."

1. The sun sets in the west. _____

2. The "big dipper" moves across the sky. _____

3. The leaves turn from green to red. _____

4. The sun is right overhead at noon. _____

5. Flowers burst into bloom. _____

REACHING OUT

Look at the two figures below. Beneath each figure, tell whether it shows rotation or revolution. Explain your answer.

Figure D

Figure E

_____

_____

_____

_____

What causes day and night?

equinox [EE-kwuh-nahks]:   day on which the sun shines directly on the equator
Northern Hemisphere: the part of the earth north of the equator
solstice [SAHL-stis]:   day on which the North Pole points toward or away from the sun
Southern Hemisphere: the part of the earth south of the equator

LESSON 11 | What causes day and night?

Usually when you go to sleep, it is dark. You wake up the next morning, and it is light. Several hours will pass and day will change to night again.

What causes day and night? The changes of day and night are caused by the earth's rotation.

As the earth rotates, only one half faces the sun at any given time. The half that is facing the sun has day. The opposite side (the side that is facing away from the sun) has night.

As the earth rotates, new parts face the sun. Places that have night slowly turn to day. One complete rotation of the earth takes 24 hours. In most places, therefore, one change from night to day and then back to night again takes 24 hours.

How many of these 24 hours are night? How many are day? It depends upon two things: the time of year, and how far from the equator a place is.

If the earth's axis were vertical (straight up and down), all parts of the earth would have 12 hours day and 12 hours night all year-round. But, the earth's axis is not vertical. The earth's axis is tilted 23 1/2 degrees.

As the earth moves around the sun, the tilt of the earth does not change. The earth just changes its position compared to the sun. Sometimes the earth is tilted so that the northern portion of the earth is facing the sun. This makes the days longer than nights in the **Northern Hemisphere.**

When the earth moves to the other side of the sun, the southern portion of the earth is facing the sun. Now the days are longer than nights in the **Southern Hemisphere.**

How far north and south of the equator a place is, also affects how long day and night will be. The farther north or south of the equator a place is, the greater the difference in length there is between day and night.

UNDERSTANDING DAY AND NIGHT

Study Figure A. Then answer the questions or fill in the blanks.

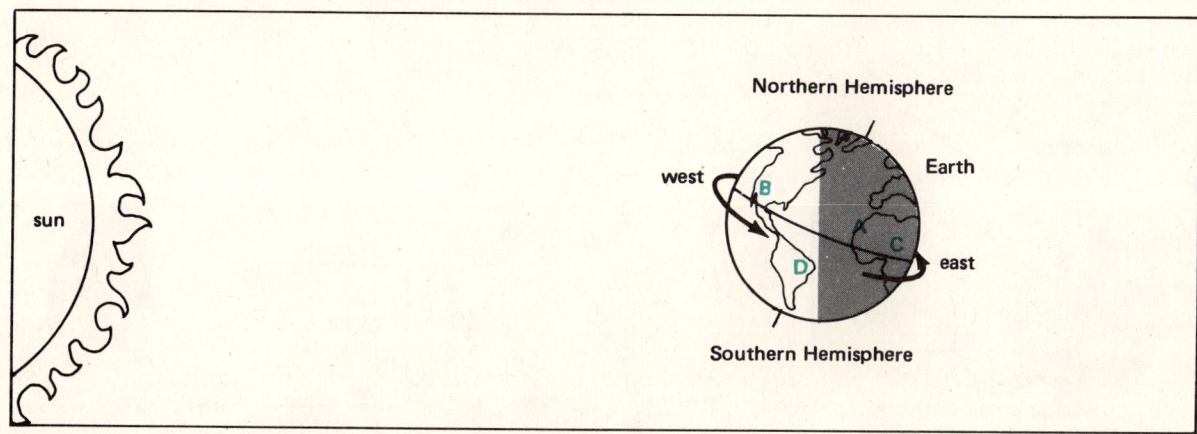

Figure A

1. The earth turns on its axis. Another way of saying this is the earth

   _____ on its axis.
   _{revolves, rotates}

   revolves, rotates

2. How many hours does one rotation of earth take? _____

3. At any given time,

   a) how much of the earth is facing the sun?_____

   b) how much of the sun is facing away from the sun? _____

4. The part of the earth facing the sun has _____ .

   night, day

5. The part of the earth facing away from the sun has _____ .

   night, day

6. The earth rotates from _____ .

   east to west, west to east

A, B, C, and D are places on the earth.

7. **a)** Which of these places are having day? _____

   b) Which of these places are having night? _____

8. Of the places that are having day, which one will move into night first?_____

9. Of the places that are having night, which one will move into day first?_____

10. **a)** Which places are in the Northern Hemisphere? _____

    b) Which place is in the Southern Hemisphere?_____

THE LONG AND SHORT OF IT

Study Figure B. Answer the questions or fill in the blanks.

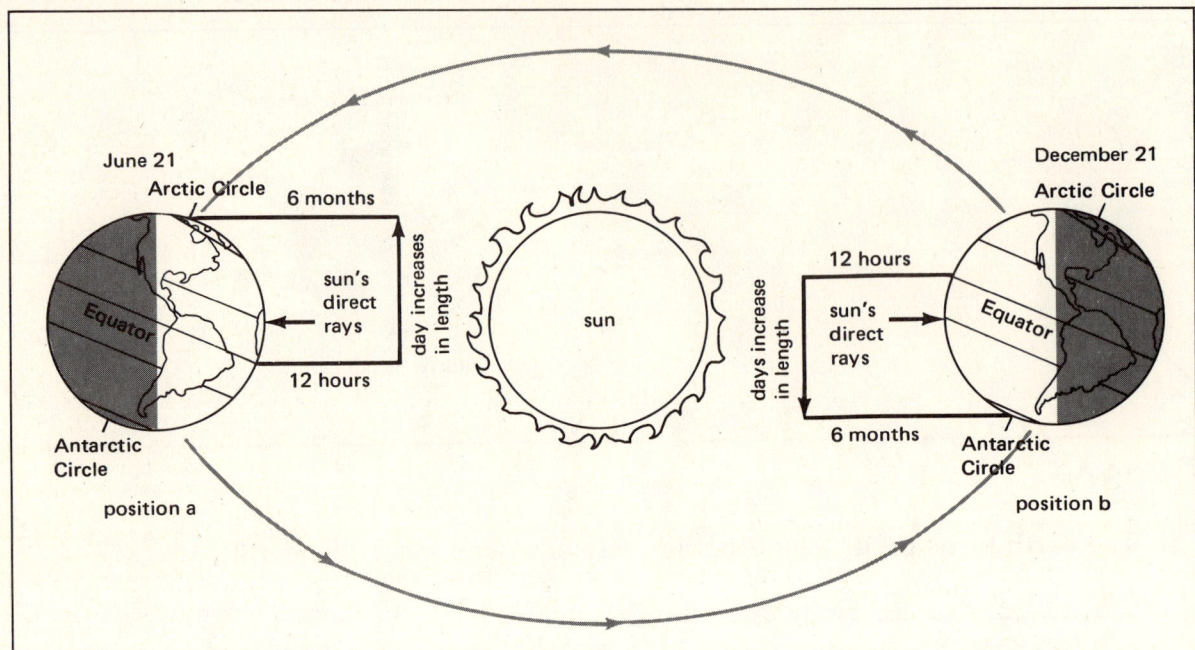

Figure B

Position a shows the earth on June 21.

Position b shows the earth six months later on December 21. It has now come halfway along its revolution around the earth.

1. Look at the earth's axis on both dates. Has the angle of its tilt compared to the sun

   changed? _____

2. Has the direction of the tilt compared to the sun changed? _____

JUNE 21

On June 21, the North Pole points directly toward the sun. This day in the Northern Hemisphere is the summer **solstice** [SAHL-stis]. On this day the North Pole has 24 hours of sunlight.

1. On June 21, the _____ Hemisphere tilts toward the sun.
   Northern, Southern

2. On June 21, the _____ Hemisphere tilts away from the sun.
   Northern, Southern

3. On June 21, the _____ Hemisphere has more hours of sunlight.
   Northern, Southern

4. On June 21, the _____ Hemisphere has fewer hours of sunlight.
   Northern, Southern

5. On June 21, days are longer in the _____ Hemisphere.

   _{Northern, Southern}

   Northern, Southern

6. If days in the Northern Hemisphere are longer, then days in the Southern Hemi-

   sphere are _____ .

   longer, shorter

7. On June 21, the _____ has 12 hours of day and 12 hours of night.

   equator, arctic circle, antarctic circle

8. As you move farther north, the days become _____ .

   longer, shorter

9. On June 21, there are _____ hours of daylight in the Arctic circle.

   zero, 12, 24

10. When it is day at the Arctic Circle, it is _____ at the Antarctic Circle.

DECEMBER 21

On December 21, the North Pole points away from the sun. This day in the Northern Hemisphere is the winter solstice. On this day, the North Pole has 24 hours of darkness.

1. On December 21, the _____ Hemisphere leans toward the sun.

   Northern, Southern

2. On December 21, the _____ Hemisphere leans away from the sun.

   Northern, Southern

3. On December 21, the _____ Hemisphere has more hours of sunlight.

   Northern, Southern

4. On December 21, the _____ Hemisphere has fewer hours of

   Northern, Southern

   sunlight.

5. On December 21, days are longer in the _____ Hemisphere.

   Northern, Southern

6. If days in the Southern Hemisphere are longer, then days in the Northern

   Hemisphere are _____ .

   longer, shorter

7. On December 21, the _____ has 12 hours of day and 12 hours of night.

   equator, arctic circle, antarctic circle

8. The length of day and night _____ seem to change at the equator.

   does, does not

9. On December 21, there are _____ hours of daylight in the Antarctic Circle.

   zero, 12, 24

10. When it is day at the Antarctic Circle it is _____ at the Arctic Circle.

For most of the year, the number of hours of day and night in the Northern and Southern Hemispheres are unequal.

On just two days of the year, every place on earth has an equal number of hours of day and night.

On March 21 and September 21, neither hemisphere leans towards the sun. On these days, every place on earth has 12 hours of daylight and 12 hours of darkness.

March 21 and September 21 are called **equinoxes** [EE-kwuh-nahks-ez].

Figure C shows the earth during one revolution around the sun. Study Figure C. Then answer the questions or fill in the blanks.

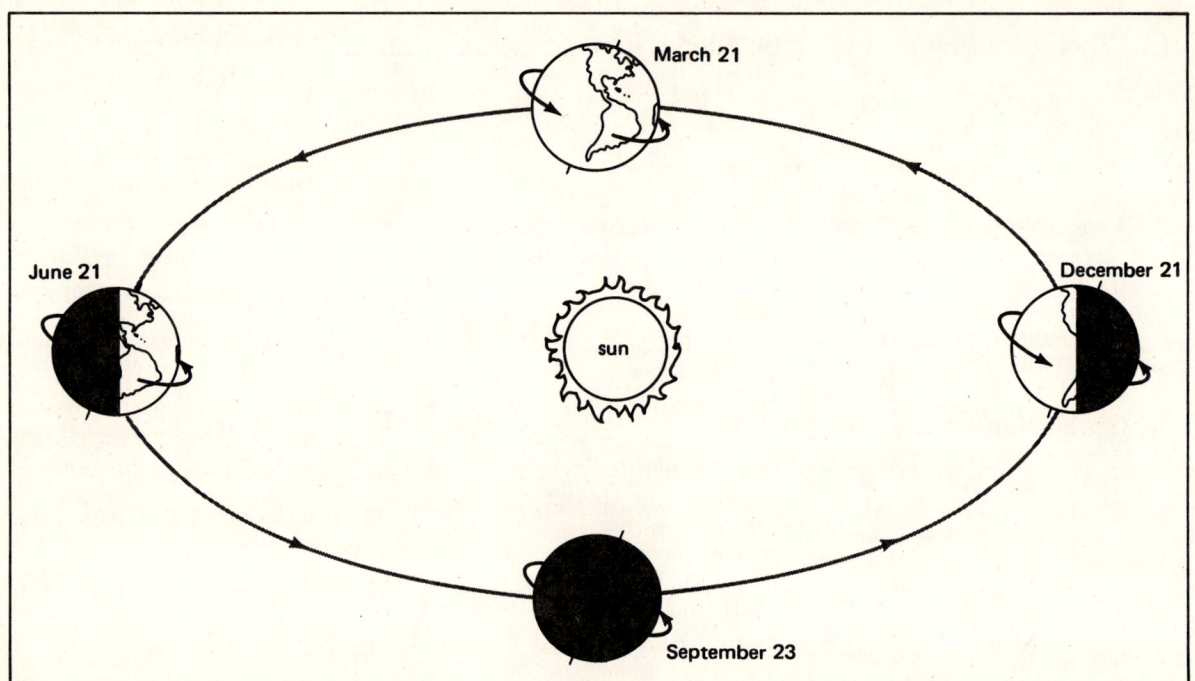

Figure C

1. The earth _____ on its axis.

rotates, revolves

2. The earth _____ around the sun.

rotates, revolves

3. One rotation makes one _____.

day, year

4. One revolution makes one _____.

day, year

5. Look at the earth's axis on each date.

   a) Has the angle changed? _____

   b) Has the axis changed the way it leans toward or away from the sun? _____

NAME THE DATES

1. The Northern Hemisphere leans toward the sun most on _____ .

2. The Northern Hemisphere leans away from the sun most on_____ .

3. The earth's axis does not lean toward nor away from the sun on

    _____ and _____ .

4. The longest day of the year in the Northern Hemisphere is _____ .

5. The shortest day of the year in the Northern Hemisphere is _____ .

6. Day and night are equal in length everywhere on earth on _____

    and _____ .

7. In the Northern Hemisphere, between June 21 and September 21, days become

    _____ .
    <small>longer, shorter</small>

8. In the Northern Hemisphere, between September 21 and December 21, days become

    _____ .
    <small>longer, shorter</small>

9. In the Northern Hemisphere, between December 21 and March 21, days become

    _____ .
    <small>longer, shorter</small>

10. In the Northern Hemisphere, between March 21 and June 21, days become

    _____ .
    <small>longer, shorter</small>

11. Differences in the number of hours of day and night happen _____ .
    <small>slowly, suddenly</small>

12. In which hemisphere do you live? _____

13. What is today's date? _____

14. On this date, where you live, there will be more hours of _____ .
    <small>day, night</small>

15. Tomorrow, day will last a few minutes _____ and night will last a few
    <small>longer, shorter</small>

    minutes _____ .
    <small>longer, shorter</small>

MATCHING

Match each term in Column A with its description in Column B. Write the correct letter in the space provided.

	Column A		Column B
_____	1. earth's rotation	a)	tilt of earth's axis
_____	2. 23 1/2°	b)	fewest hours of night in the Northern Hemisphere
_____	3. December 21	c)	day and night equal everywhere
_____	4. June 21	d)	causes day and night
_____	5. March 21 and September 23	e)	most daylight hours in the Southern Hemisphere

REACHING OUT

What do we call these dates in the Northern Hemisphere? Write the names next to the dates.

December 21 _____   March 21 _____

September 21 _____   June 21 _____

What are time zones?

prime meridian [muh-RID-ee-un]: imaginary line that runs north and south through Greenwich, England

international date line: imaginary line that runs north and south and separates one day from the next

time zone: part of the earth where it is the same time; the earth has 24 time zones.

LESSON 12 | What are time zones?

When it is 12 noon in New York, it is three hours earlier, (9 A.M.) in California. At the same moment in Paris, France, it is five hours later (5 P.M.).

Why is the time different around the world?

Time depends upon the earth's rotation. The earth rotates from west to east once every 24 hours. As it rotates, the sun seems to move from east to west.

Because of this, places in the east see the sun before places in the west.

- It is later in the day in places that have already seen the sunrise.
- It is earlier in places that are waiting to see the sun.

New York, for example, is east of California. The sun rises in New York three hours before it rises in California. California must still wait three hours for the sun to rise. Therefore, it is three hours earlier in California than it is New York.

How do we know how many hours difference there are between places?

The earth is divided into 24 standard **time zones**. They are imaginary lines that run north and south. The starting line is called the **prime meridian** [muh-RID-ee-un]. Distance between zones is measured in degrees east or west of the prime meridian.

There is one hour difference between each time zone. For each zone to the <u>east</u>, you <u>add</u> one hour. For each zone to the <u>west</u>, you <u>subtract</u> one hour.

Here's an example. If it is 10 A.M. where you live, then the time in the zone just to the east is 11 A.M. The time zone just to the west is 9 A.M.

Study Figure A. Then answer the questions or fill in the blanks. A through F stand for different places.

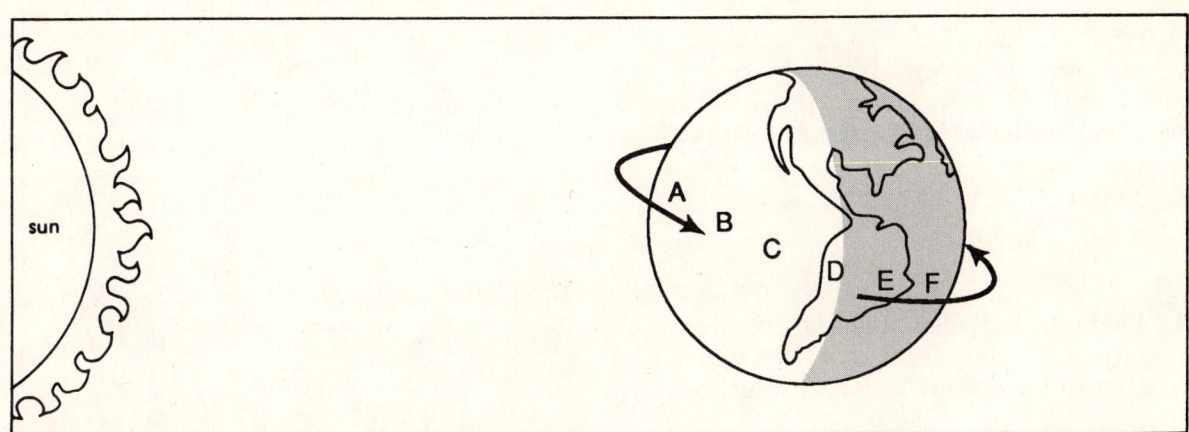

Figure A

1. List the places that are having day: _____

2. Which of these places had day first? _____

3. Which of these places had day last? _____

4. In which direction does the earth rotate? _____
   west to east, east to west

5. As you go to the west, the time becomes _____ .
   earlier, later

6. As you go to the east, time becomes _____ .
   earlier, later

7. B is _____ of C. The time at B is _____ than the time at C.
   east, west earlier, later

8. B is _____ of A. The time at B is _____ than the time at A.
   east, west earlier, later

9. List the places that are having night: _____

10. Which of these places had night first? _____

11. Which of these places had night last? _____

12. E is _____ of D. The time in E is _____ than the time in D.
    east, west earlier, later

13. E is _____ of F. The time at E is _____ than the time at F.
    east, west earlier, later

14. Of all the places in the diagram, where is it the earliest? _____

15. Of all the places in the diagram, where it it the latest? _____

Figure B shows the meridians. Study Figure B. Then answer the questions or fill in the blanks.

1. The direction that meridians travel

   is _____ .

   north and south, parallel with the equator

2. The prime meridian passes through

   what city in England? _____

   _____

3. Distance between meridians is measured in degrees (°). How many degrees are there between meridians? _____

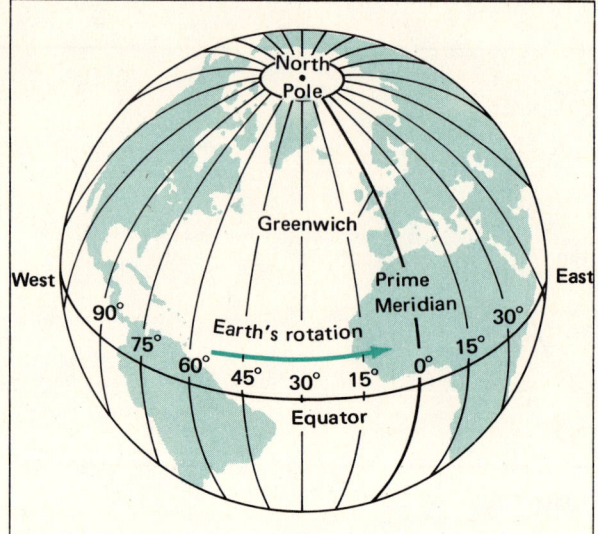

Figure B

The meridians in Figure B are straight lines. The angle between meridians are all the same. But the time zones do not look this way.

Most time zones are not straight lines. They zigzag in order to keep certain related places within the same time zone.

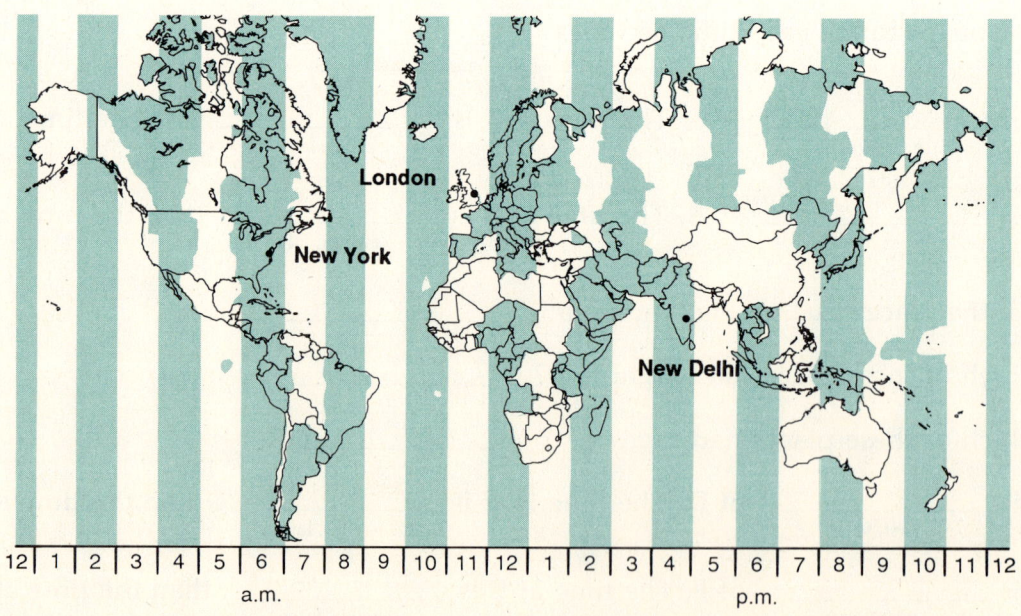

Figure C

4. New York is _____ of the prime meridian.
   east, west

5. How many hours difference is there between London and New York? _____

6. The time in London is _____ than the time in New York.
   earlier, later

7. When it is 2 P.M. in New York, what time is it in London?_____

8. When it is 6 A.M. in London, what time is it in New York?_____

9. When it is 1 P.M. in London, what time is it in New Delhi?_____

10. When it is 12 noon in New Delhi, what time is it in London? _____

NORTH AMERICA'S TIME ZONES

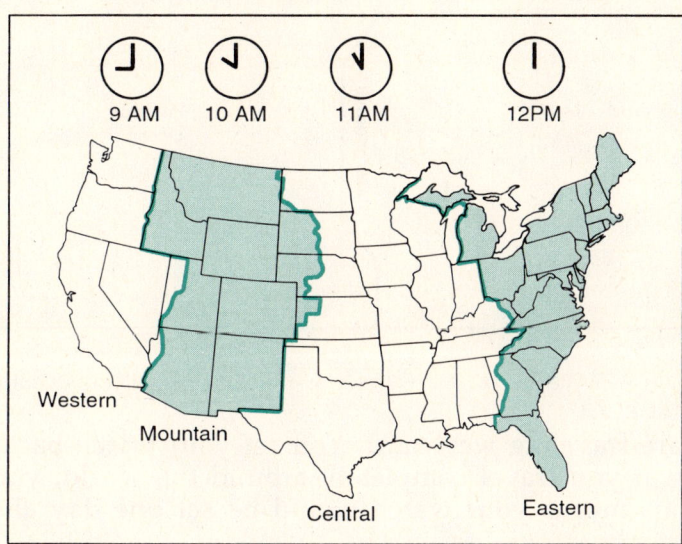

Figure D

Figure D shows the United States. It is divided into four time zones. Study the figure. Answer the questions.

1. Name the time zones in North America.

   _____   _____

   _____   _____

2. When it is 2 P.M. in the Eastern zone, it is _____ in the Mountain zone.
   12 P.M., 1 P.M., 4 P.M.

3. When it is 4 A.M. in the Pacific zone, it is _____ in the Mountain zone.
   3 A.M., 4 A.M., 6 A.M.

4. When it is midnight in the Central zone, it is _____ in the Pacific zone.
   12 A.M., 1 A.M., 2 A.M.

5. When it is midnight in the Central zone, it is _____ in the Eastern zone.
   11 P.M., 12 A.M., 2 A.M.

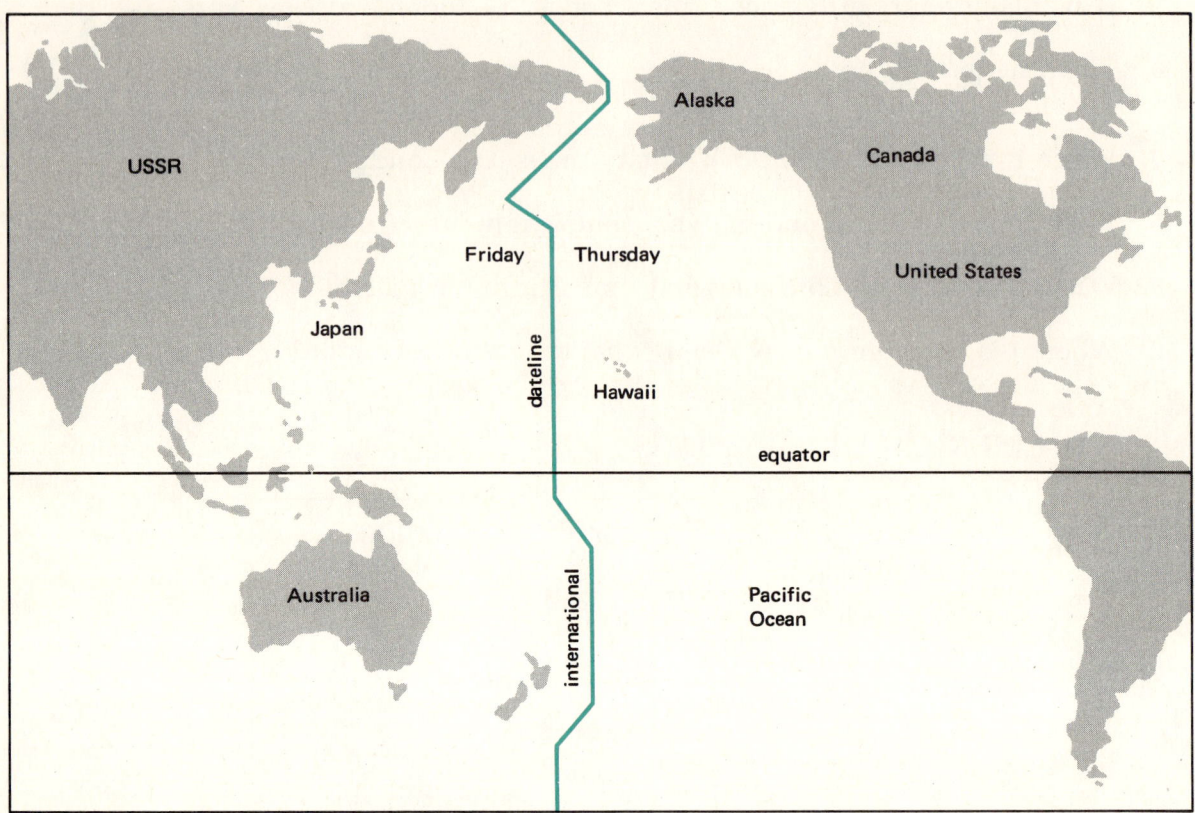

Figure E

Imagine that you are traveling westward. You set your watch back one hour for each meridian you pass. If you travel completely around the world, you will change your watch 24 times. This means your watch would be set one day ahead of every else's watches.

To correct this problem, people agreed that when they crossed a certain meridian, they would change the time on their watches by one day, just like they change their watches by one hour when they enter a new time zone. They called this imaginary line the **international date line.** The international date line is set at the 180° meridian, halfway around the world from the prime meridian.

When you cross the international date line from <u>east to west</u> you <u>add</u> one day. Sunday, for example, becomes Monday.

When you cross the international date line from <u>west to east</u>, you <u>subtract</u> one day. Sunday becomes Saturday.

Now answer these questions:

1. When it is Tuesday in the United States, what day it is in Japan?_____

2. When it is Wednesday in Australia, what day is it in Alaska? _____

3. When it is Friday in Hawaii, what day is it in Canada? _____

COMPLETING SENTENCES

Choose the correct word or term for each statement. Write your choice in the spaces provided.

1. Time depends upon the earth's _____ .
   revolution, rotation

2. The sun seems to move across the sky from _____ .
   west to east, east to west

3. Places in the west see the sun _____ places in the east.
   before, after

4. The time in the west is _____ than the time in the east.
   earlier, later

5. The time in the east is _____ than the time in the west.
   earlier, later

6. The earth is divided into _____ time zones.
   12, 24, 60

7. Time zones run _____ .
   vertically, horizontally

8. The starting time line is called the _____ .
   prime meridian, international date line

9. The time difference between time zones is one _____ .
   day, hour, year

10. For each time zone to the east, you _____ one hour.
    add, subtract

11. For each time zone to the west, you _____ one hour.
    add, subtract

12. The number of degrees between time zones is _____ .
    90, 15, 180

13. The date changes when you cross the _____ .
    prime meridian, international date line

14. It is a day later when you cross the international date line from

    _____ .
    west to east, east to west

15. It is a day earlier when you cross the international date line from

    _____ .
    west to east, east to west

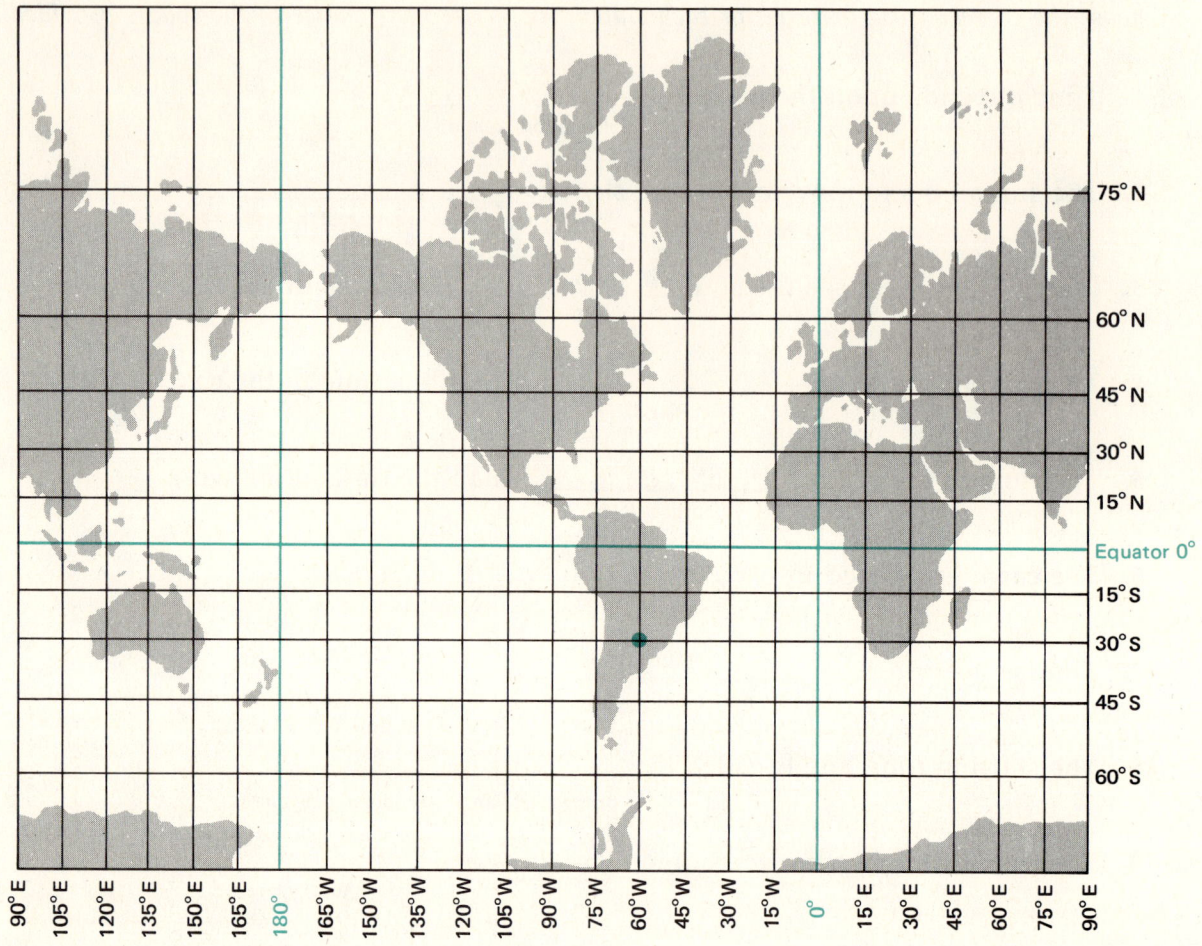

Figure F

The meridians divide the earth into time zones. But they also tell us how far east or west a place is. Location east or west is measured in degrees of longitude.

There are also imaginary lines that run parallel to the equator. These are lines of latitude. They tell us how far north or south of the equator a place is in degrees of latitude.

Look at Figure F. It shows the lines of latitude and longitude. Find the dot that marks the location of 30° south latitude and 60° west longitude. This may be written as 30° S latitude; 60° W longitude.

Now find each of the following locations. Mark each with a dot and its number.

1. 30° S latitude; 245° E longitude

2. 60° N latitude; 105° W longitude

3. 60° N latitude; 75° E longitude

4. 15° N latitude; 105° E longitude

5. 0° S latitude; 15° W longitude

6. 45° N latitude; 90° W longitude

How does the earth orbit the sun?

13

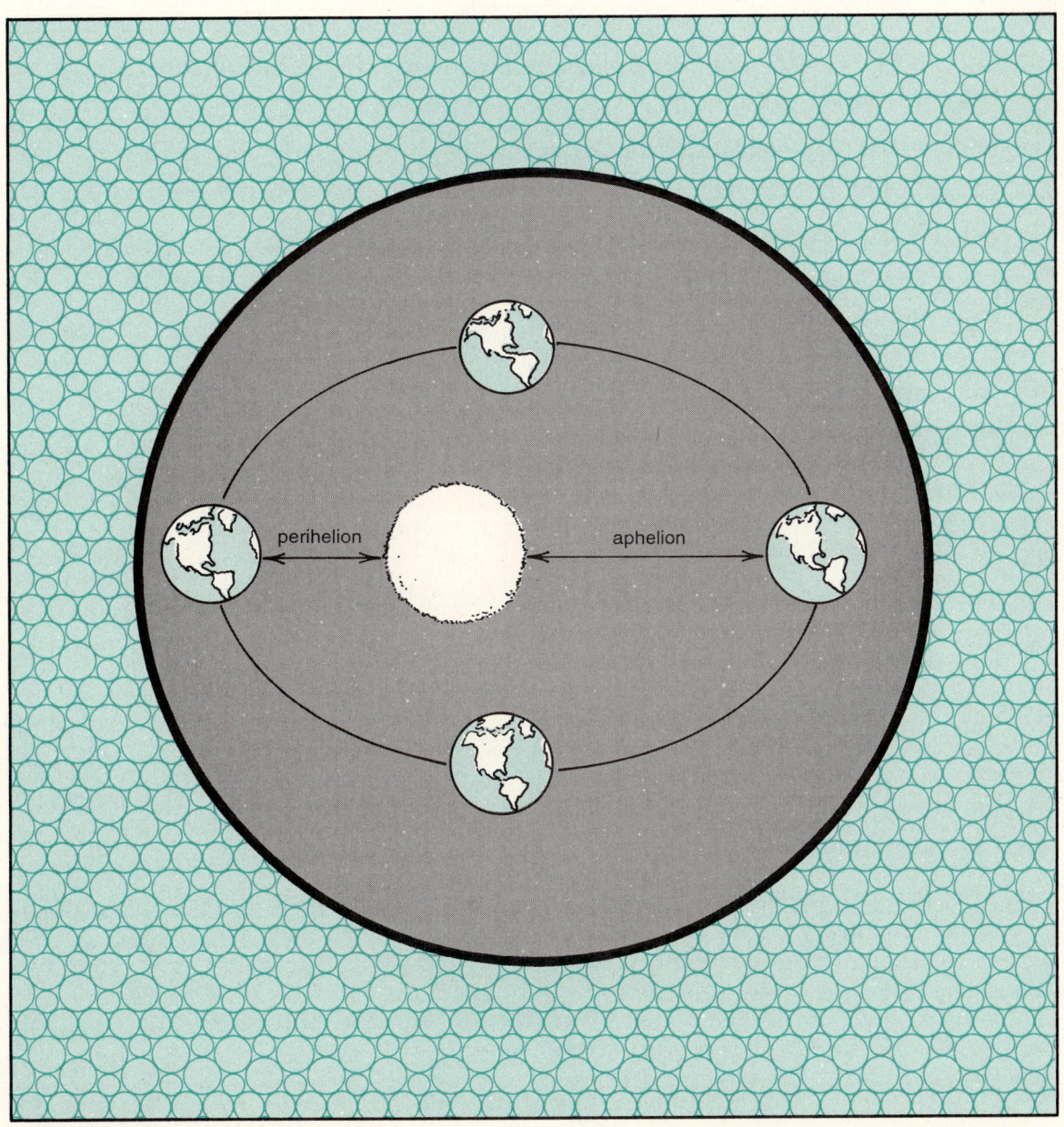

aphelion [af-FEEL-yun]:   point in the earth's orbit where the earth and sun are the farthest apart
ellipse [uh-LIPS]:   oval-shaped
gravity [GRAV-uh-tee]:   force of attraction that exists between all objects in the universe
perihelion [per-uh-HEEL-yun]:   point in the earth's orbit where the earth and sun are the closest

LESSON 13 | How does the earth orbit the sun?

Look at Figure A on the facing page. By now, you know it well. It shows the earth's orbit around the sun.

Notice that the earth's orbit is not in the shape of a circle. The earth's orbit is slightly oval-shaped. This shape is called an **ellipse** [uh-LIPS].

What is the difference between a circle an an ellipse?

In a circle, the distance from the center to any point along the edge is the same.

In an ellipse, the distance from the center to the edge changes as you move along the edge.

An ellipse has a long axis and a short axis. They cross at right angles at the center of the ellipse.

The earth's orbit is an ellipse. And the sun is not exactly in the center of the ellipse. It is slightly off center. For these reasons, the earth is not the same distance from the sun at all times.

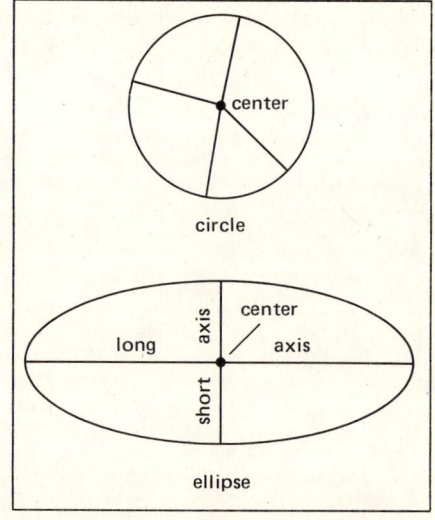

About January 2, the earth is closest to the sun. It is about 147 million kilometers away. The point in the orbit that is closest to the sun is called the **perihelion** [per-uh-HEEL-yun].

About July 3, the earth is farthest from the sun. It is about 152 million kilometers away. The point in the orbit that is farthest from the sun is called the **aphelion** [af-FEEL-yun].

All the planets—not just the earth—orbit the sun in elliptical paths.

THE EARTH'S ORBIT AROUND THE SUN

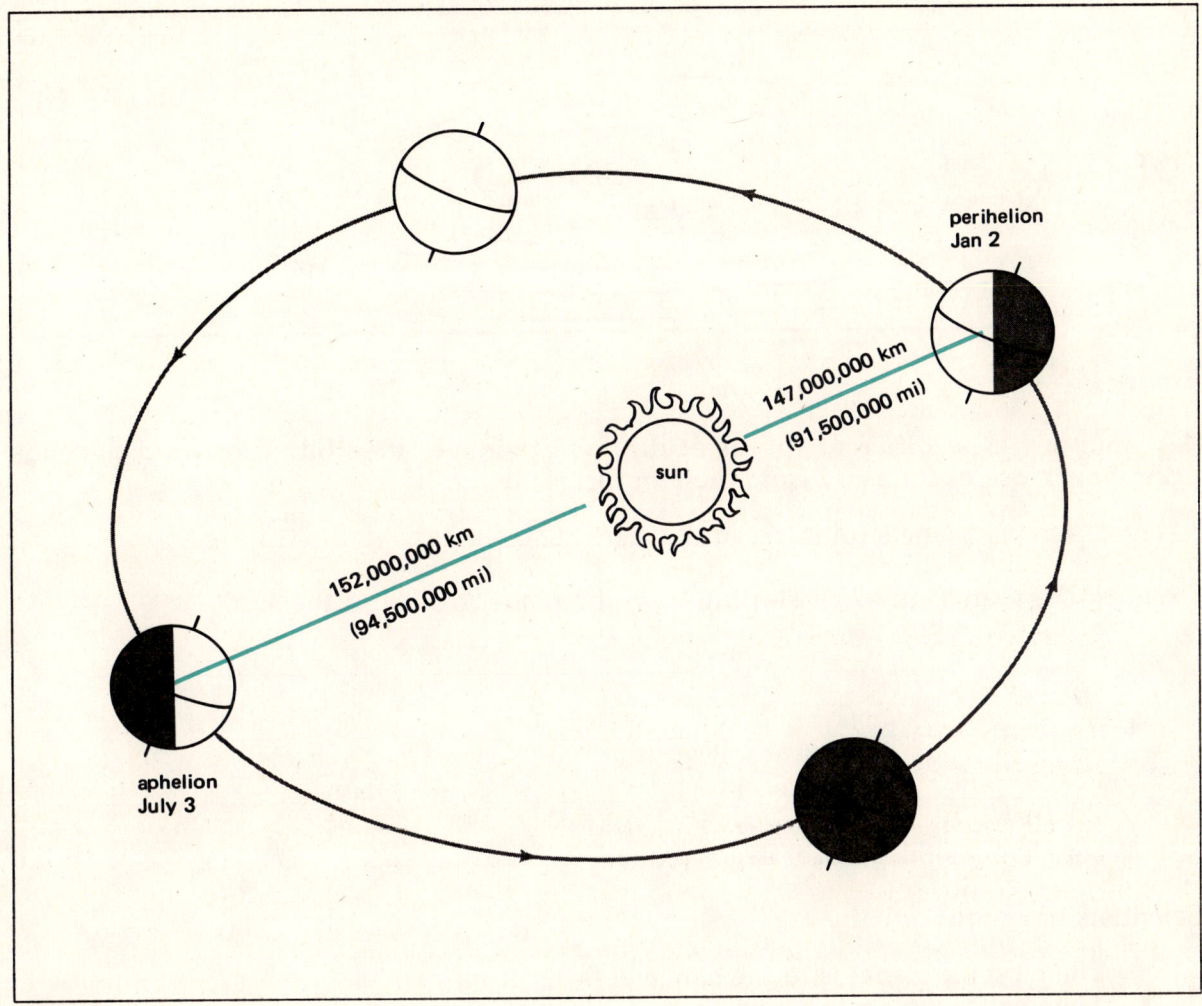

Figure A

1. What is the shape of the earth's orbit?_____

2. Is the sun in the center of the orbit? _____

3. Is the earth the same distance from the sun along the entire orbit?_____

4. How far is the earth from the sun about January 2? _____

5. This is the earth's _____ distance from the sun.
    _{closest, farthest}

6. What do we call this point of the earth's orbit? _____

7. How far is the earth from the sun about July 3? _____

8. This is the earth's _____ distance from the sun.
    _{closest, farthest}

9. What do we call this point of the earth's orbit? _____

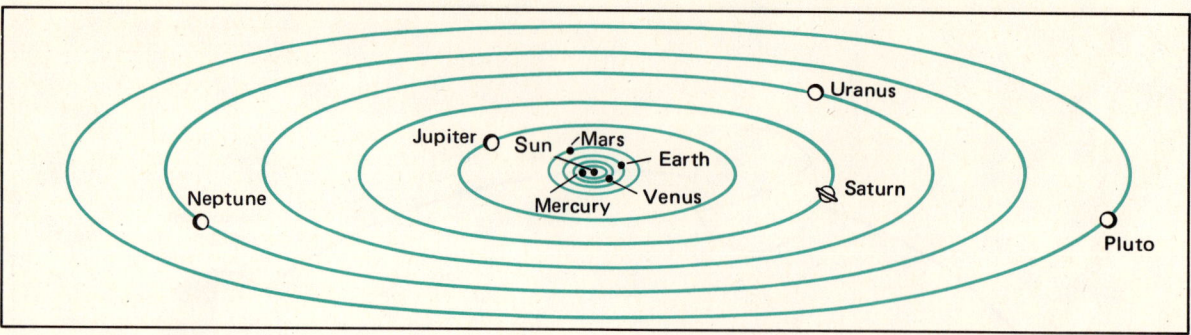

Figure B

A planet moves at different speeds at different points of its orbit. The speed depends upon how close or far away from the sun the planet is.

1. How many planets orbit the sun? _____

2. List the planets in order starting with the planet closest to the sun.

    (1) _____   (2) _____   (3) _____

    (4) _____   (5) _____   (6) _____

    (7) _____   (8) _____   (9) _____

3. What shape is the orbit of every planet? _____

Scientists have found that:

*   The <u>closer</u> a planet is to the sun, the <u>faster</u> it moves.
*   The <u>farther</u> a planet is from the sun, the <u>slower</u> it moves.

The speed of a planet's orbit is called its orbital velocity [OR-buh-tul vuh-LOS-uh-tee]

4. **a)** Which planet has the slowest orbital velocity? _____

    b) Why? _____

5. **a)** Which planet has the fastest orbital velocity? _____

    b) Why? _____

A planet moves at different speeds at different points of its orbit. The speed depends upon how close or far away from the sun the planet is.

6. Look back at Figure A.

    a) On which date does the earth move the fastest? _____

    b) Why? _____

7. **a)** On which date does the earth move the slowest? _____

    b) Why? _____

GRAVITY

You throw a ball into the air. It moves upward for a short time. Then it starts falling back to the ground. Why does it fall back? Why doesn't it keep moving upward? A force called gravity pulls it back toward the earth. **Gravity** is a pulling force. It is the force that attracts objects toward one another.

Gravity pulls the earth and anything on the earth towards one another. As you stand on the earth, you are pulled downward, toward the center of the earth.

Every object in the universe pulls on every other object in the universe, from the tiniest atom to the largest star. However, all objects do not have the same gravitational pull. The strength of a gravitational pull depends upon two things. They are the:

AMOUNT OF MATTER in the objects pulling each other. The more matter there is, the stronger the pull. The pull of an atom is tiny. The pull of a star is huge.

DISTANCE between the objects. The closer two objects are to each other, the more they pull on each other. The pull of Earth on you is very large since you are so close to Earth. The pull of Jupiter on you is smaller since Jupiter is so far away.

Gravity holds the planets around the sun and moons around the planets. If there were no gravity the planets would just fly off into space away from the sun.

FILL IN THE BLANK

Complete each statement using a term or terms from the list below. Write your answers in the spaces provided.

matter	moon	downward
sun	gravity	distance between
pulling		

1. The force that pulls objects towards one another is called _____ .

2. Gravity is a _____ force.

3. Gravity pulls things on the earth _____ .

4. Gravity depends upon two things: the amount of _____ objects

   have, and the _____ the objects.

5. Gravity keeps the _____ moving around the Earth. It also keeps

   the planets moving around the _____ .

TRUE OR FALSE

In the space provided, write "true" if the sentence is true. Write "false" if the sentence is false.

_____ 1. The planets move in circular orbits around the sun.

_____ 2. The sun is in the very center of the earth's orbit.

_____ 3. The earth is at the same distance from the sun at all times.

_____ 4. The earth's orbital velocity changes as it moves around the sun.

_____ 5. Aphelion is the closest point of an orbit.

_____ 6. Perihelion is the closest point of an orbit.

_____ 7. The earth is at aphelion in July.

_____ 8. The earth is closest to the sun in July.

_____ 9. The closer a planet is to the sun, the faster it moves.

_____ 10. The orbital velocity of Pluto is faster than the orbital velocity of Earth.

REACHING OUT

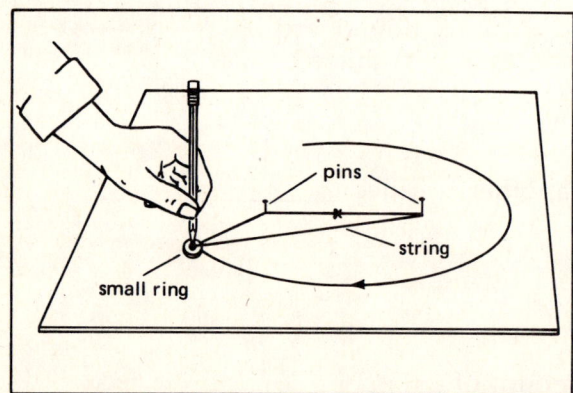

Figure C

You can make an ellipse easily. Figure C shows how to do it.

Make a few ellipses at home.

Try using different string lengths and different pin positions.

What causes the change of seasons?

14

direct rays: light rays that hit the earth straight on
indirect rays: light rays that do not hit the earth straight on

LESSON 14 | What causes the change of seasons?

Are you ready for a vacation? Will you go swimming or will you go ice-skating? Of course, it all depends on the season.

Most people live in places that have four seasons—spring, summer, autumn, and winter.

The four seasons are marked by differences in temperature and in the lengths of day and night.

Summer, for example, is much warmer than winter. And summer days are longer than winter days.

What causes seasons? Seasons are caused by the earth's revolution around the sun and the unchanging tilt of the earth's axis.

You have already learned how the earth's axis causes differences in the lengths of day and night. The axis also causes differences in temperature.

Part of the year, the axis leans towards the sun. Part of the year, the axis leans away from the sun.

For example, June 21 is the first day of summer in the Northern Hemisphere. On that day, the Northern Hemisphere leans toward the sun the most. The sun's rays strike head-on or nearly head-on over a large part of this hemisphere.

Direct rays are rays that are head on. Direct rays are strong rays. They do not spread over a large area. Direct rays heat up the earth the most.

December 21 is the first day of winter in the Northern Hemisphere. On that day, the Northern Hemisphere leans away from the sun the most. The sun's rays do not strike head-on. They spread over a large area.

Rays that spread out are called **indirect rays**. Indirect rays are weak rays. They heat up the earth the least.

UNDERSTANDING DIRECT AND INDIRECT RAYS

Figure A shows direct rays and indirect rays. Study it. Then answer the questions or fill in the blanks.

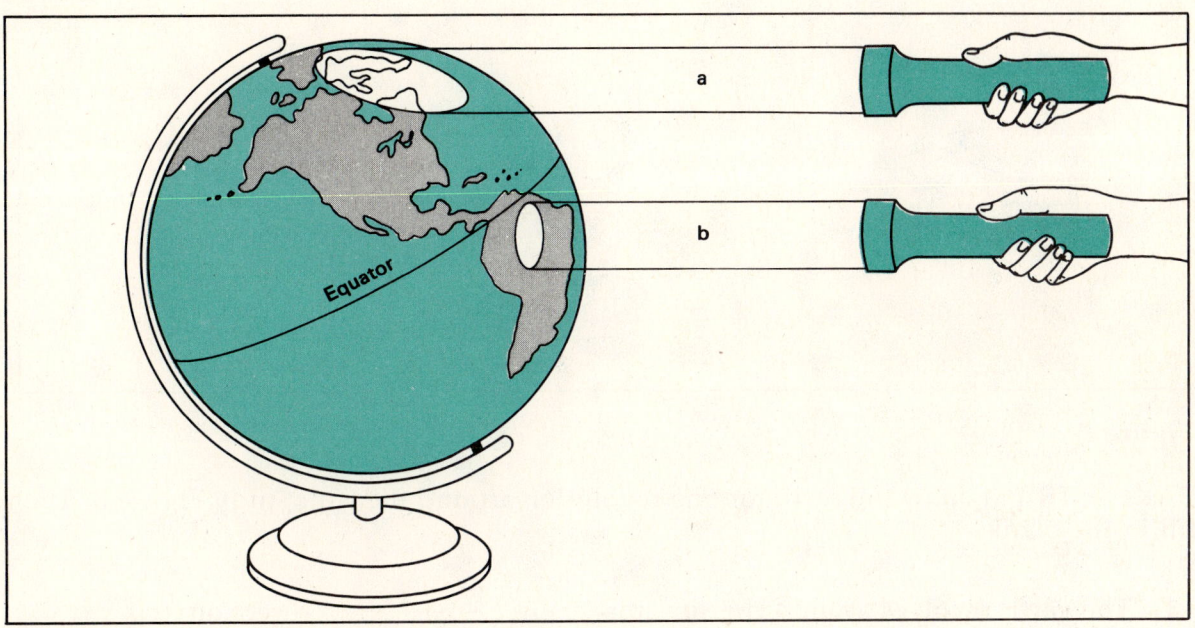

Figure A

1. Which rays are direct? _____

a, b

2. Which rays are indirect? _____

a, b

Answer "direct" or "indirect".

3. Which rays spread out? _____

4. Which rays do not spread out? _____

5. Which rays are stronger? _____

6. Which rays are weaker? _____

7. Which rays heat a place more? _____

8. Which rays heat a place less? _____

9. Winter rays are _____ rays.

10. Summer rays are _____ rays.

11. Which of the rays of Figure A can stand for winter rays? _____

a, b

12. Which of the rays on Figure A can stand for summer rays? _____

a, b

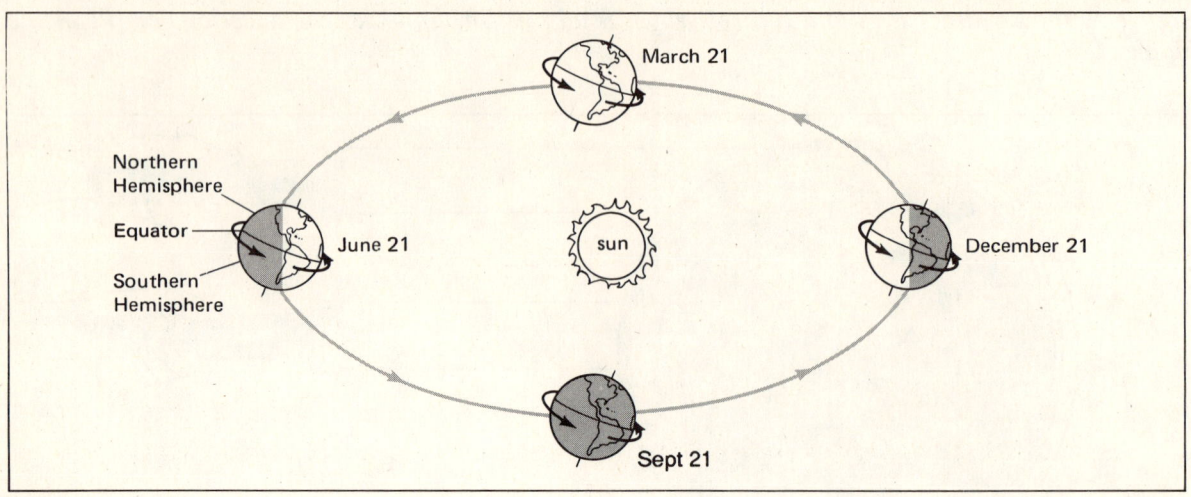

Figure B

TAKE A TRIP. Follow the earth for one revolution around the sun. Study Figure B. Then fill in the blanks.

1. The earth revolves around the sun in a _____ direction.

clockwise, counterclockwise

2. As the earth revolves around the sun, the earth's axis _____ change.

does, does not

3. **On June 21, the Northern Hemisphere . . .**

   a) faces _____ the sun.

toward, away from

   b) has mainly _____ weather.

cold, warm

   c) has _____ hours of daylight than the Southern Hemisphere.

more, fewer

   d) receives _____ rays. These are _____ rays.

direct, slanting   *strong, weak*

   e) has the first day of _____ .

summer, fall, winter, spring

4. **Between June 21 and September 20, . . .**

   a) the Northern Hemisphere still leans toward the sun, but every day the lean

   becomes _____ .

greater, less

   b) the rays become _____ direct and spread out _____ .

more, less   *more, less*

   c) the days become _____ and the nights become _____ .

longer, shorter   *longer, shorter*

5. **On September 21 . . .**

   a) the earth's axis is tilted _____ the sun.

toward, away from, neither toward nor away from

   b) the sun's rays are _____ .

direct, indirect, neither direct nor indirect

   c) _____ starts in the Northern Hemisphere.

summer, fall, winter, spring

   d) every place on Earth has _____ hours of day and

   _____ hours of night.

6. **Between September 21 and December 20 . . .**

   a) the Northern Hemisphere starts to lean _____ the sun.

toward, away from

   b) the sun's rays become more _____ . These rays are

direct, indirect
   _____ .

stronger, weaker

   c) days become _____ and nights become _____ .

longer, shorter ... longer, shorter

7. **On December 21 the Northern Hemisphere . . .**

   a) faces _____ the sun.

toward, away from

   b) has mainly _____ weather.

cold, warm

   c) has _____ hours of daylight than the Southern Hemisphere.

more, fewer

   d) receives _____ rays. These are _____ rays.

direct, indirect ... strong, weak

   e) has the first day of _____ .

summer, fall, winter, spring

8. **Between December 21 and March 20 . . .**

   a) the Northern Hemisphere leans away from the sun, but every day the lean

   becomes _____ .

more, less

   b) the rays become _____ slanting.

more, less

   c) the days become _____ and the nights become _____ .

longer, shorter ... longer, shorter

9. **On March 21 . . .**

a) the earth's axis is tilted _____ the sun.

toward, away from, neither toward nor away from

b) the sun's rays are _____ .

direct, indirect, neither direct nor indirect

c) _____ starts in the Northern Hemisphere.

summer, fall, winter, spring

10. **Between March 21 and June 21 . . .**

a) the Northern Hemisphere starts to lean _____ the sun.

toward, away from

b) the rays become more and more _____ .

direct, indirect

c) the rays become _____ .

stronger, weaker

d) the days become _____ and the nights become _____ .

longer, shorter · longer, shorter

11. In the Northern Hemisphere, the number of daylight hours is greatest on

_____ ; this is the first day of _____ .

March 21, June 21, September 23, December 20 · summer, fall, winter, spring

CONGRATULATIONS! YOUR TRIP AROUND THE SUN IS NOW COMPLETE!

12. How long did your trip take? _____

REACHING OUT

Record-breaking temperatures rarely happen on the first day of summer. It is usually the later months of summer that have the hottest weather. Why?

_____

_____

_____

_____

What is known about the earth's moon?

15

craters [KRAY-turz]:   round holes on the moon's surface
lunar: related to the moon
maria [MAHR-ee-uh]:   broad, flat plains on the moon
meteorite [MEE-tee-or-ite]:   piece of rock or metal that hits the earth's surface

LESSON 15 | What is known about the earth's moon?

"That's one small step for a man — one giant leap for mankind."

The date was July 20, 1969. And with those historic words, astronaut Neil Armstrong became the first person to set foot on the moon. For two hours, he and fellow astronaut, Edwin Aldrin, walked on its surface. They took pictures, collected rocks, and performed experiments.

Altogether, twelve astronauts (all American), have explored the moon's surface. Several scientific instruments were left behind. They sent back valuable moon data.

To the unaided eye, the moon's surface, also called the **lunar** surface, seems little more then patches of light and dark areas. However, with a telescope, we can see a variety of features. Three of the most noticeable features are <u>maria</u>, <u>craters</u>, and <u>mountains</u>.

MARIA   Galileo, the famous astronomer, studied the moon through his telescope. He thought the basins were filled with water — and named them **maria** [MAHR-ee-uh]. *Maria* is the Latin word for seas.

Lunar "seas" are not seas at all. They contain no water. In fact, there is no water <u>or</u> air on the moon . . . None at all! Lunar "seas" are really broad and generally smooth <u>plains</u>. They look dark because their dark rock reflects less light than surrounding high areas. The lunar maria were formed from hardened lava flows.

Now we know that these "seas" are dry. But the name remains. Actually, both terms are used — <u>seas</u> and <u>maria</u>.

CRATERS   **Craters** [KRAY-turz] are impressions on the moon's surface. They are generally round with rugged rims.

Craters are formed when **meteorites** [MEE-tee-or-ites] impact upon the moon's surface. The entire moon's surface — even the maria are pocked with craters. In fact, some craters have even smaller craters.

Craters vary in size — from microscopic size to ones several hundred feet across. More than 30,000 craters have been mapped. If we included the very tiny ones, there would be too many to count.

MOUNTAINS   Lunar mountains, are, indeed, MOUNTAINS. Some tower 18,000 feet — and more. The tallest lunar mountain is 1,930 meters (26,000 feet) high. That's nearly 5 miles.

Figure A

"That's one small step for a man, one giant leap for mankind." Neil Armstrong said these words as he became the first person to set foot on the moon. Figure A shows a photo that Armstrong took of his fellow astronaut, Edwin Aldrin.

If you look closely at Aldrin's visor, you can see the reflection of Neil Armstrong taking the picture.

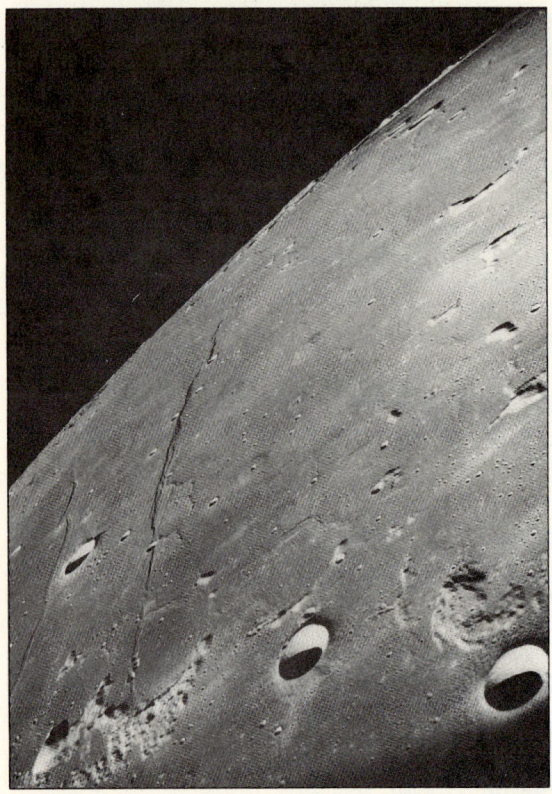

Figure B

The moon's surface is constantly bombarded by meteorites. When meteorites hit the moon, impact craters are formed. In some places on the moon, there are so many craters that new craters simply cover up old craters. When lava formed the lunar maria, it covered up all the craters that had previously been there. As a result, the maria only have craters from meteorites which struck the moon after the lava hardened. Therefore, there are fewer craters in the maria.

Meteorites constantly enter the earth's atmosphere as well. Yet almost all burn up in the atmosphere long before they could crash onto the surface.

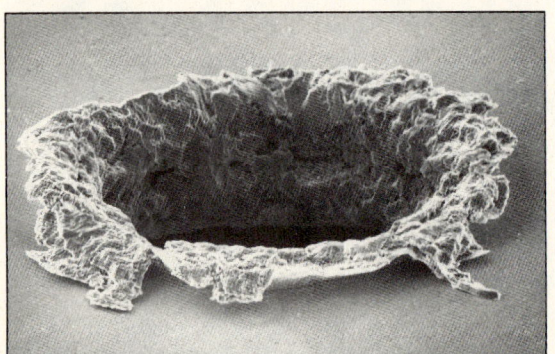

Figure C

Meteorites can be any size. Some are very very small. Even tiny micrometeorites can form craters. They impact at speeds of up to 40 kilometers (64 miles) per second surface. This never ending "sandblasting" pits the moon's surface.

Figure D

Impacts from meteorites break up some of the moon's rock into a fine dust. The moon's surface is covered with this fine grey-brown dust.

TRUE OR FALSE

In the space provided, write "true" if the sentence is true. Write "false" if the sentence is false.

_____   **1.** A telescope makes things larger.

_____   **2.** Galileo is a modern-day scientist.

_____   **3.** Lunar seas contain water.

_____   **4.** The Moon can support life.

_____   **5.** Craters on the Moon were formed by meteorite impacts.

_____   **6.** All lunar seas have craters.

_____   **7.** Lunar seas show up as light patches.

_____   **8.** Lunar craters can be found in many sizes.

FILL IN THE BLANK

Complete each statement using a term or terms from the list below. Write your answers in the spaces provided.

lava	maria	craters
round	moon	sizes
smooth	micrometeorites	flat
meteorites		

1. The earth's only natural satellite is the _____ .

2. Lunar maria are dry areas that are generally _____ and

   _____ .

3. Another name for lunar "seas" is _____ .

4. Depressions that dot the lunar surface are called _____ .

5. Lunar "seas" were formed from hardened _____ .

6. Highly visible lunar craters were caused by impacting _____ .

7. Craters are generally _____ and are found in a great range of

   _____ .

8. The tiniest craters are caused by the impact of _____ .

MATCHING

Match each term in Column A with its description in Column B. Write the correct letter in the space provided.

	Column A		Column B
_____	1. telescope	**a)**	molten volcanic material
_____	2. maria	**b)**	useful scientific tool
_____	3. crater	**c)**	rock material from space
_____	4. lava	**d)**	lunar seas
_____	5. meteorite	**e)**	created by meteorite impacts

REACHING OUT

Figure E *A photo of the moon taken by Apollo 17 astronauts.*

We now know for certain. The moon has no air and no water. Do you think there is life

on the moon? Why? _____

_____

Why can we see only one side of the moon?

16

apogee [AP-uh-jee]:   point at which the moon is farthest from the earth
perigee [PER-uh-jee]:   point at which the moon is closest to the earth

LESSON 16 | Why can we see only one side of the moon?

On August 10, 1956, an Atlas Agena rocket blasted off from Kennedy Space Flight Center. It carried an unmanned satellite—Lunar Orbiter 1. Four days later, Orbiter 1 was circling the moon. This satellite sent back many pictures. Some showed the back half of the moon.

From the earth, we can see only one side of the moon. The other side of the moon always faces away from us.

Why does only one side of the moon face us? The explanation is really simple.

Like the earth, the moon rotates. That is, it turns around its own axis. While the moon is rotating, it is also revolving. It is moving around the earth.

• One moon rotation takes 27 1/3 days.

• One moon revolution takes the same time—27 1/3 days.

The periods of rotation and revolution are the same. The moon turns around its center once for each time it moves around the earth.

Because of this, only one side of the moon faces us. The opposite side always is hidden from the earth.

UNDERSTANDING ROTATION

Have you ever seen a top spinning? How about a gymnast doing a flip? Both of these motions involve rotation. Rotation is the spinning of an object around its axis. The moon also rotates around its axis.

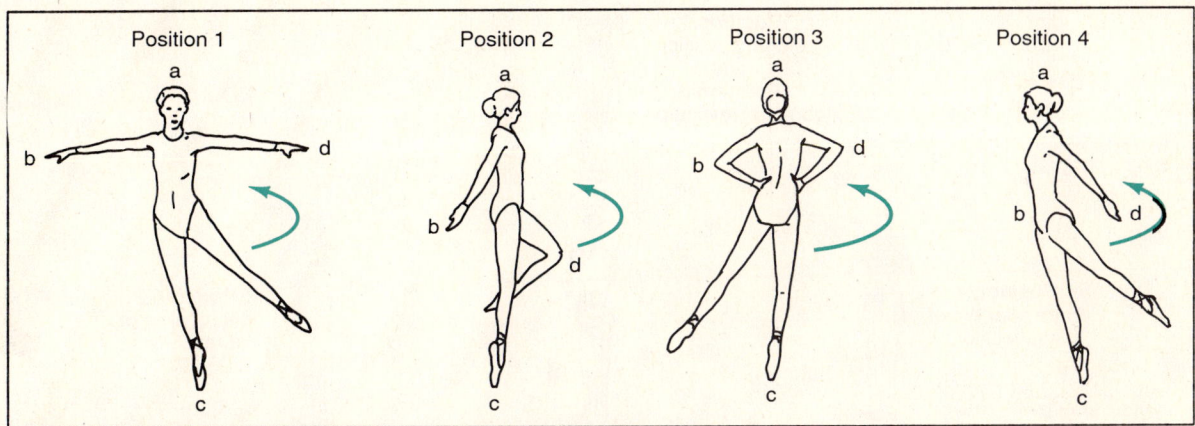

Figure A *Rotation*

Imagine you are the dancer in Figure A. During one rotation, you will face in every direction of the circle. At the end of one rotation, you will face the same direction as when you started.

1. List the points you expect to see as you turn. _____

2. Will you see the places between these points? _____

3. After one quarter turn, which point do you see?_____

4. After two one-quarter turns, which point do you see? _____

5. Two one-quarter turns equals which fraction of one turn?_____

   1/4, 1/2, 3/4

6. Look at your starting position. At one half turn, the direction you face is

   _____ .

   the same, just opposite

7. At three one-quarter turns, which point do you see?   _____

8. Three one-quarter turns equals which fraction of one turn?   _____

   1/4, 1/2, 3/4

9. When you make one more quarter turn, which point do you see again?_____

10. a) Did you rotate? _____

    b) Did you revolve? _____

    c) How do you know? _____

    _____

91

UNDERSTANDING REVOLUTION

Revolution is the movement of an object all the way around another object.

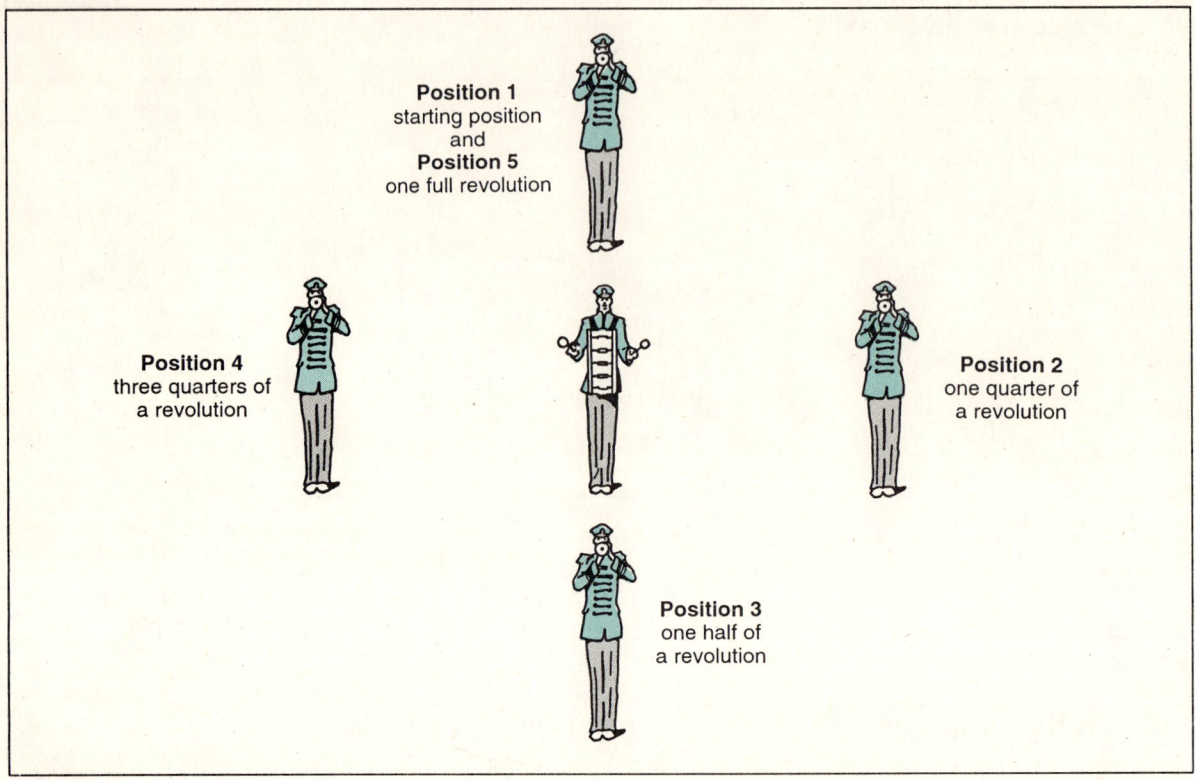

Position 1
starting position
and
Position 5
one full revolution

Position 4
three quarters of
a revolution

Position 2
one quarter of
a revolution

Position 3
one half of
a revolution

Figure B *Revolution*

Figure B shows a trumpet player revolving around a drum player. The trumpet player is playing his trumpet while he is revolving. He always faces towards the audience. He faces forward. Imagine you are the trumpet player in Figure B. Answer the following questions.

1. After one quarter revolution, what will you see? _____

2. After one half of a revolution, what will you see? _____

3. After three quarters of a revolution, what will you see? _____

4. After one full revolution, what will you see? _____

5. Did you always face the same direction? _____

6. Did you rotate? _____

7. Did you travel all the way around the drummer? _____

8. Did you revolve? _____

9. When an object revolves, can it also rotate? _____

10. When an object revolves, must it also rotate? _____

UNDERSTANDING REVOLUTION AND ROTATION TOGETHER

Imagine that you are walking (revolving) around a chair. The diagram below shows what you look like.

Study the diagram. Then answer the questions.

Figure C *Rotation and Revolution together*

1. How many revolutions have you made?_____

2. At half way through the revolution, you were facing _____
   the opposite, the same

   direction as when you started.

3. At one revolution, you were facing _____ direction as when you started.
   the opposite, the same

4. What were you doing while you were revolving? _____

5. How many times? _____

6. As you were revolving and rotating, how many sides of your body faced the chair?

   _____
   one, two, three, all

7. When an object rotates once for each time it revolves around an object

   _____.
   only one side faces the object, all sides face the object

APOGEE AND PERIGEE

The moon revolves around the earth in an elliptical orbit at a speed of 3500 kilometers per hour. It takes 27 1/3 days to make one complete revolution.

The point in the orbit where the moon is farthest from the earth is called **apogee** [AP-uh-jee]. The distance from the moon to the earth during apogee is 409,000 kilometers. The point in the orbit where the moon is closest to the earth is called **perigee** [PER-uh-gee]. The distance from the moon to the earth during perigee is 365,000 kilometers.

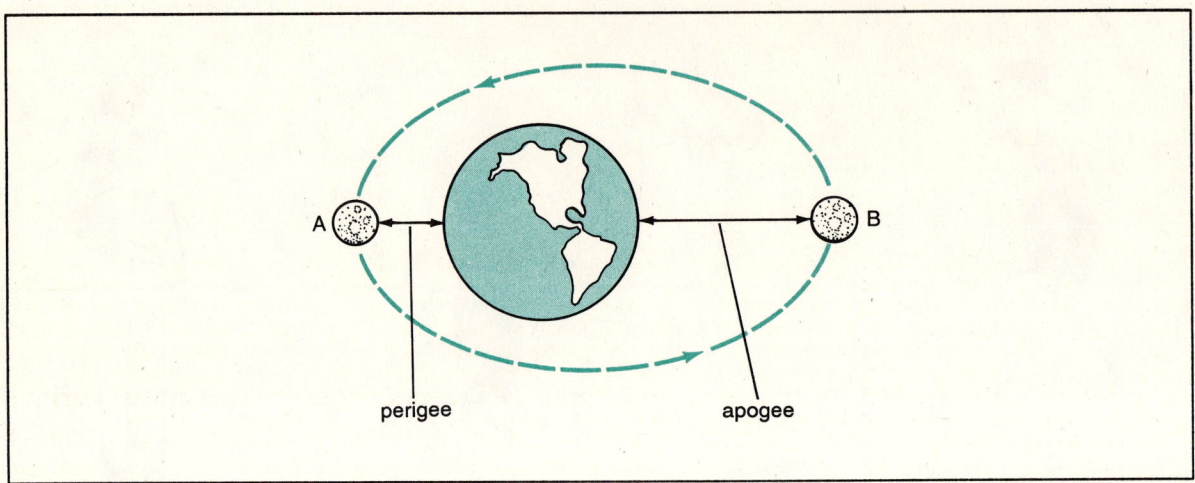

Figure D

Use Figure D to answer the following questions.

1. When the moon is closest to the earth, it is at _____.

2. When the moon is farthest fron the earth, it is at_____.

3. The moon takes _____ days to make one complete revolution around the earth.

4. The moon takes _____ days to make one complete rotation on its axis.

5. Why does the same side of the moon always face the earth? _____

_____

_____

NOW TRY THIS

Use the diagram to complete the following.

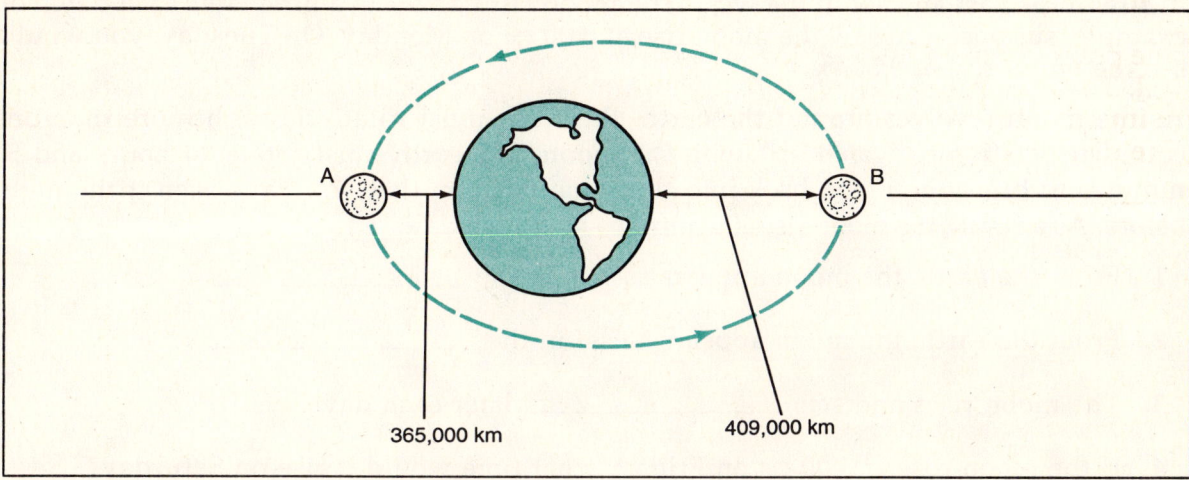

Figure E   *The elliptical orbit of the moon.*

1. The diagram shows the distance of the moon from the earth at apogee and at perigee. Label each of these positions on the diagram in the space provided.

2. What is the distance of the moon from the earth at apogee? _____

3. What is the distance of the moon from the earth at perigee? _____

4. How much closer to the earth is the moon at perigee than at apogee?

   _____

MATCHING

Match each term in Column A with its description in Column B. Write the correct letter in the space provided.

	Column A		Column B
_____	1. apogee	**a)**	when the earth is closest to the moon
_____	2. perigee	**b)**	spinning of an object around its axis
_____	3. revolution	**c)**	moon related
_____	4. rotation	**d)**	when the earth is farthest from the moon
_____	5. lunar	**e)**	movement of an object around another

MOON RISE AND MOON SET

The earth's rotation brings the moon into view every day. Like the sun, the moon appears to rise in the east and set in the west. The moon rises and sets a little later each day. For example, suppose you saw the moon rise at 8:00 PM on Monday. On Tuesday, you would see the moon rise at 8:50 PM.

As the moon revolves around the earth, the earth must rotate through more than one complete rotation to "catch up" with the moon. The earth must rotate 24 hours and 50 minutes to bring the moon back into the same position that you have seen it the night before. As a result, the moon rises 50 minutes later each day. .

1. From the earth, the moon appears to rise in the _____ .

2. From the earth, the moon appears to set in the _____.

3. The moon rises and sets _____ later each day.

4. If the moon rose at 5:00 PM on Friday, what time would it rise on Saturday?

    _____

5. If the moon set at 5:30 AM on Wednesday, what time would it set on Thursday?

    _____

REACHING OUT

The word "month" comes from a variation of the Greek word meaning "moon." Use a dictionary or other reference source and find out how the word "month" got its name. Write this information in the space provided.

_____

_____

_____

_____

_____

What are the phases of the moon?

phases [FAYZ-uz]: changing shapes of the moon
waning [WAYN-ning]: after the full moon; as the visible part of the moon decreases
waxing: after a new moon; as the visible part of the moon increases

LESSON 17 | What are the phases of the moon?

The moon does not give off its own light like the sun does. It shines by reflected light. The sun shines on the moon. The moon then reflects this light from the sun to our eyes.

You can see the moon shining brightly on almost any clear night. But from night to night, the moon seems to change its shape. The different shapes the moon seems to have are called **phases** [FAYZ-uz]. Figure A shows the phases.

If you look at the moon every night, you will notice that the phases always follow one another in the same order. First the moon may look like a large white disk. Then it seems to shrink and disappear only to start "growing" again.

Why does the moon seem to change shape? The moon revolves, or orbits, around the earth. One orbit takes about 27 1/3 days. During this time, about half of the moon is always lit up. But, most of the time we cannot see all this light.

How much moonlight we see depends upon where the moon is in its orbit. At full moon, we see all of the lit side. At new moon, we see none of the lit side. At all other phases, we see part of the lit side.

UNDERSTANDING THE MOON'S PHASES

Figure A shows the moon in orbit. Study it and then answer the questions or fill in the blanks below.

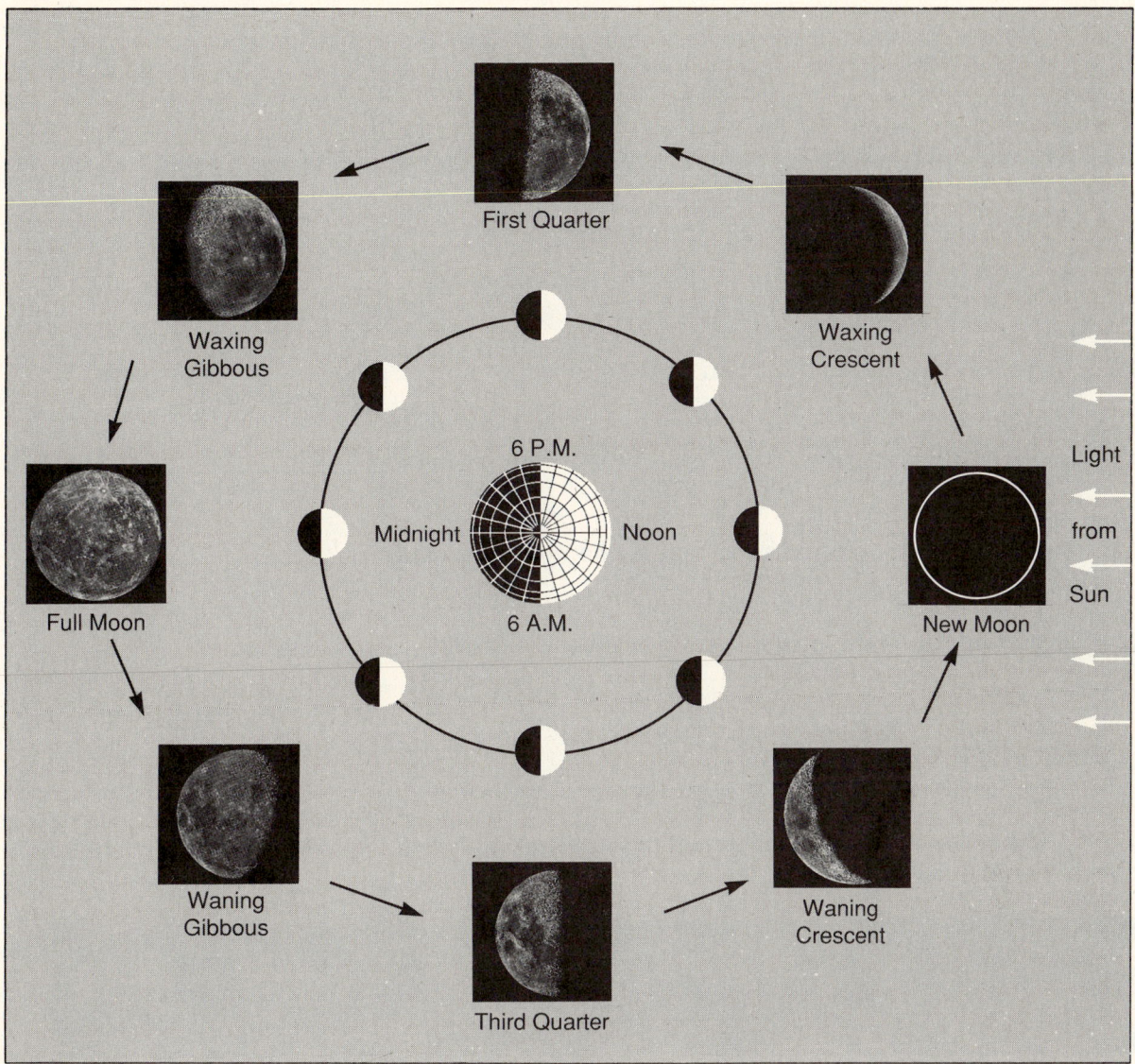

Figure A

The side of the moon facing the sun is always lit up. But we cannot see all of this lit up area every night. The boxes show how the moon looks to us from the earth. Notice how its shape seems to change during the orbit.

1. What do we call the different shapes the moon seems to have? _____

2. Where does the moon get its light? _____

3. How much of the moon is always bright? _____

4. Can we see all this light every night? _____

5. At which phase can we see <u>all</u> of the lighted half of the Moon? _____

6. At which phase can we see none of the lighted half of the Moon?_____

7. At which phases can we see one half of the lighted half of the Moon?

   _____ _____

8. At which phases can we see less than one half of the lighted part of the Moon?

   _____ _____

9. At which phases can we see more than one half, but not all of the lighted half of the

   Moon. _____ _____

10. At new moon, the lighted half of the moon faces _____ the earth.
    <small>towards, away from</small>

11. At full moon, the lighted half of the moon faces _____ the earth.
    <small>towards, away from</small>

12. Between new moon and full moon the moon seems to _____ in size.
    <small>grow, shrink</small>

13. Between full moon and new moon, the moon seems to _____ in size.
    <small>grow, shrink</small>

14. How long does the moon take to orbit the earth? _____

COMPLETE THE CHART

The figures below show the eight phases of the Moon. Complete the chart below by writing the correct figure letter or letters in the space provided.

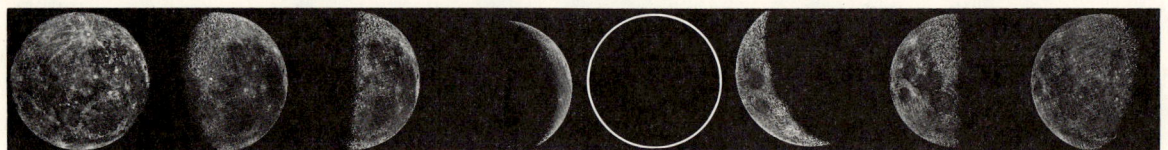

Figure B   Figure C   Figure D   Figure E   Figure F   Figure G   Figure H   Figure I

	Phase	Figure
1.	Gibbous moons	
2.	New moon	
3.	Crescent moons	
4.	Full moon	
5.	Quarter moons	

FILL IN THE BLANK

Complete each statement using a term or terms from the list below. Write your answers in the spaces provided. Some words may be used more than once.

sun	new crescent	phases
full moon	reflects	orbits
change	moon	one half
old crescent	new moon	

1. Our closest neighbor in space is the _____ .

2. The moon gets its light from the _____ . Some light from the

   moon _____ onto Earth.

3. About _____ of the moon is always bright.

4. The shape of the moon seems to _____ .

5. The different shapes that the moon seems to have ar called _____ .

6. The different shapes that the moon seems to have depend upon how much of its light

   _____ back to the Earth.

7. The moon changes appearance because it _____ the Earth.

8. At _____ we cannot see the moon.

9. At _____ we see about one whole side of the moon.

10. The phases that show least of the moon are _____ and

   _____ .

TRUE OR FALSE

In the space provided, write "true" if the sentence is true. Write "false" if the sentence is false.

_____ 1. The earth orbits the moon.

_____ 2. The moon gives off its own light.

_____ 3. The moon reflects light from the sun.

_____ 4. About one half of the moon is always lit.

_____ 5. We can always see the lit half of the moon.

Use the clues to complete the crossword puzzle.

Clues

Across

3. What the moon does around the earth

6. What the moon does to light from the sun

8. Phase of the moon when only a small part can be seen

Down

1. Revolves around the earth

2. Phase of the moon when it cannot be seen

3. Spin

4. Phase of moon when one whole side can be seen

7. Planet you are on

9. Star nearest to earth

What is a solar eclipse? 18

corona [kuh-ROH-nuh]:   outer layer of the sun's atmosphere
solar eclipse [SOH-ler uh-CLIPS]:   passing of the moon between the earth and the sun

LESSON 18 | What is a solar eclipse?

Everyone has seen shadows. You have seen shadows of trees, buildings, and fences. How often have you noticed your own shadow following you? You can see a shadow right now! Just hold your hand close to this page. What do you see on the page?

What is a shadow? A shadow is an area of darkness. It forms when an object gets in the way or blocks light.

Every object that blocks light forms a shadow. The earth and moon are no exceptions. The earth and moon block the sun's light. They cast huge cone-shaped shadows deep into space.

The earth and moon are always moving. Sometimes the earth moves behind the moon. Part of the earth is in the moon's shadow. For the people at this place on earth, the moon blocks out, or eclipses, the sun. The eclipsed area becomes dark. For a short period of time, it looks like it is night time.

A **solar eclipse** [SOH-ler uh-CLIPS] takes place when the sun, moon and Earth are in a straight or almost straight line with the moon between the sun and the Earth.

A solar eclipse does not last long — no longer than a few minutes in any one place.

Since scientists know a lot about the orbits of the Earth and the moon, they can accurately predict:

- <u>when</u> an eclipse will take place
- <u>where</u> it will take place
- <u>how long</u> it will last

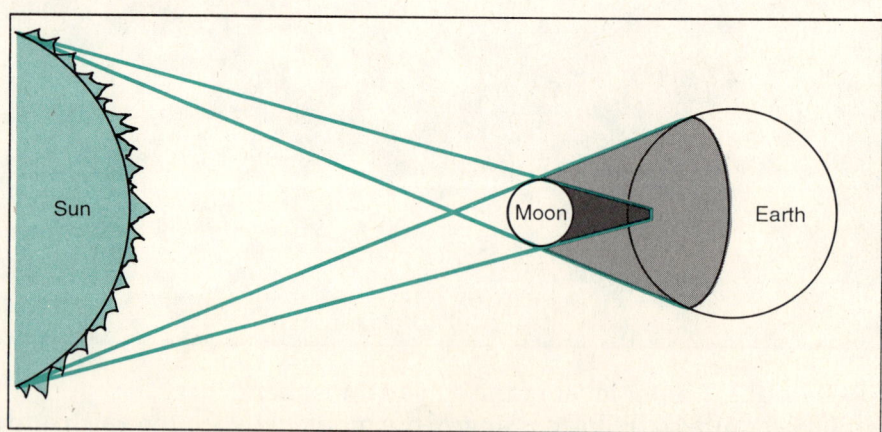

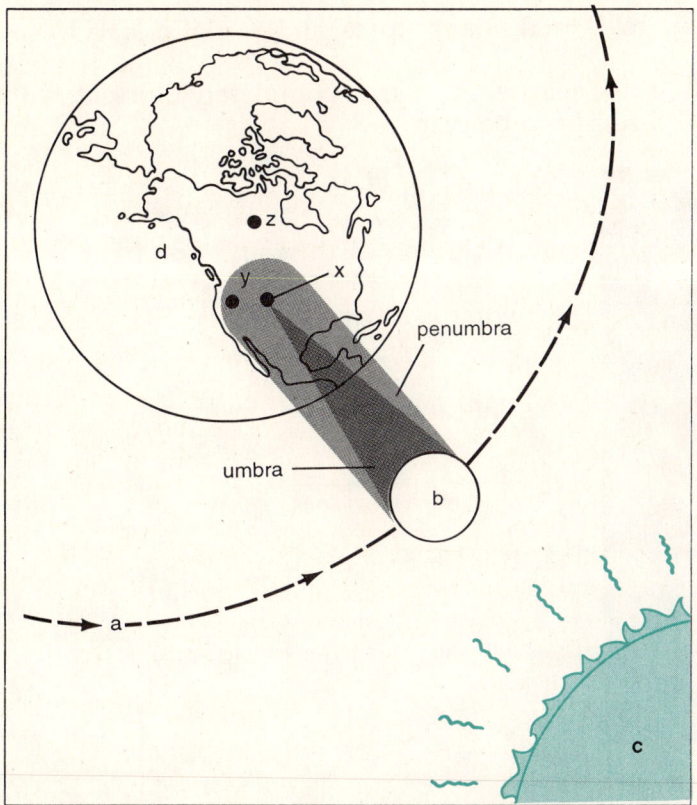

Figure A

Figure A shows a solar eclipse. Study it and answer the questions.

Identify the following by letter.

_____ 1. sun

_____ 2. earth

_____ 3. moon

_____ 4. moon's orbit

A shadow has a dark middle part, and a lighter outer part.

5. What do we call the darker middle part? _____

6. What do we call the lighter outer part? _____

7. Which part of the shadow covers a wider area?

_____

Figure B

Figure B shows a multiple exposure of a solar eclipse.

The top left shows the sun before the moon moves in front of it.

In the following images, the moon covers up more and more of the sun.

The sun then reappears at the bottom right.

TOTAL SOLAR ECLIPSES

There are two main kinds of solar eclipses — total solar eclipses, and partial solar eclipses.

Figure C shows the sun during a total solar eclipse. The sun is completely blocked. Only light from its rim or **corona** [kuh-ROH-nuh] can be seen.

Figure C   *Total solar eclipse*

Look back at Figure A.

1. Where on earth would you be to see what is shown in Figure C? _____
   x, y, z

2. This area is called the

   _____ .
   umbra, penumbra

3. It is an area of

   _____ .
   full light, reduced light, complete darkness

PARTIAL SOLAR ECLIPSE

Figure D shows the sun during a partial eclipse. Part of the sun seems "chopped off."

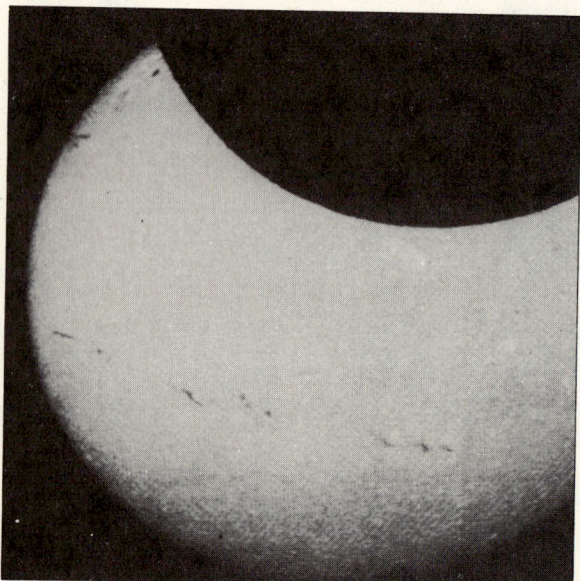

Figure D   *Partial solar eclipse*

Look back at Figure A again.

4. Where would you be to experience a partial solar eclipse? _____
   x, y, z

5. This area is called the

   _____ .
   umbra, penumbra

6. It is an area of

   _____ .
   full light, reduced light, complete darkness

7. Imagine that you are in area "z." Would you see an eclipse?_____

8. Why? _____

   _____

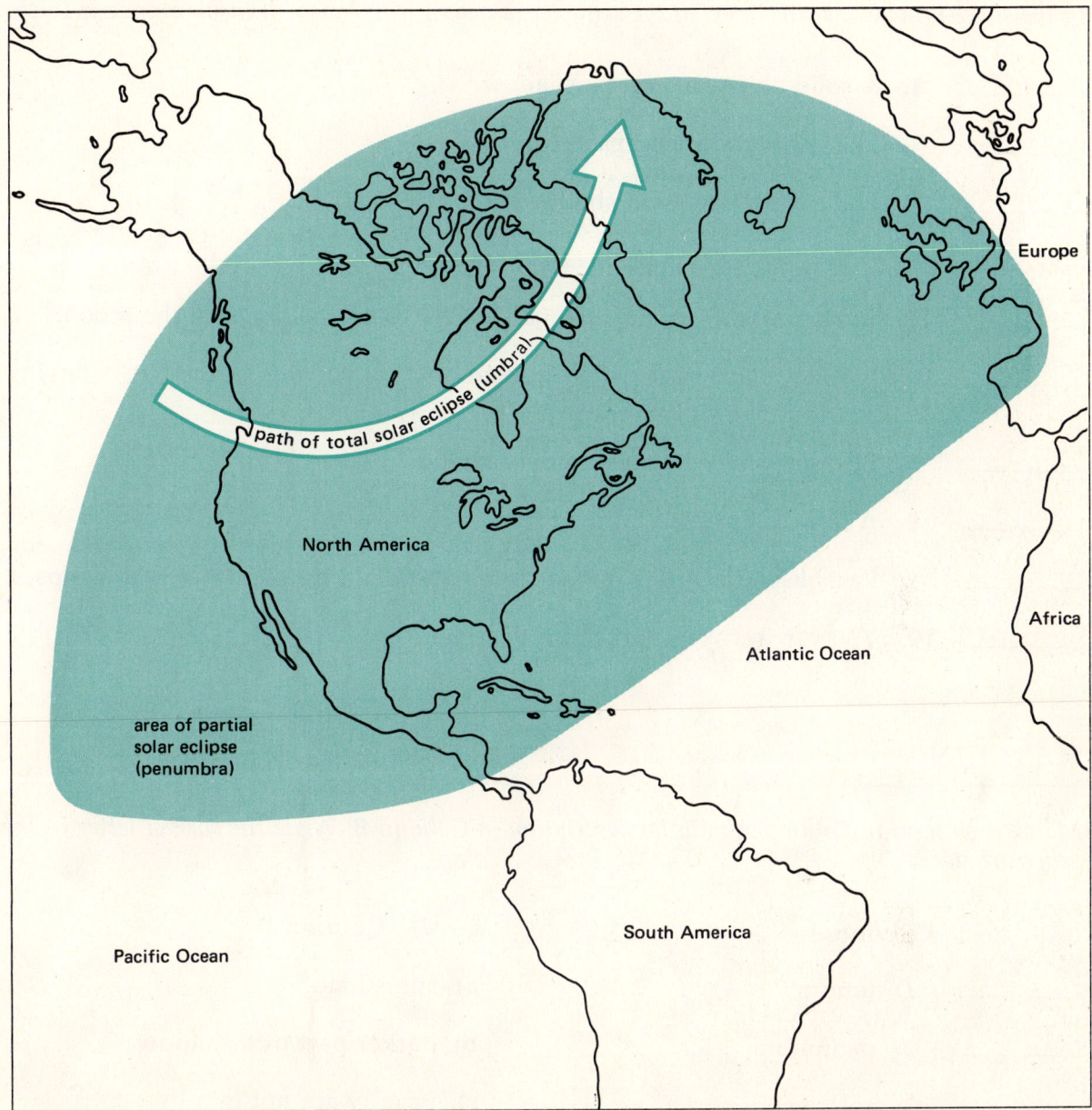

Figure E

During an eclipse, the moon moves in its orbit around the earth and the earth rotates. Therefore, the place on the surface of the earth that is in the moon's shadow changes. As the eclipse moves slowly across the earth, different people in different places see it at different times. Figure E shows the path of the total solar eclipse of February 26, 1979. The next such eclipse that can be seen from North America will be in the year 2017.

TRUE OR FALSE

In the space provided, write "true" if the sentence is true. Write "false" if the sentence is false.

_____   1. A solid object can cast a shadow.

_____   2. The earth and moon cast shadows.

_____   3. Light is needed for a shadow to form.

_____   4. During a solar eclipse, we cannot see the moon.

_____   5. During a solar eclipse, the earth is between the sun and the moon.

_____   6. A solar eclipse can be seen from any part of the earth that is having daylight at the time of the eclipse.

_____   7. The place to see a solar eclipse changes.

_____   8. A solar eclipse lasts a long time.

_____   9. Partial solar eclipses can be seen in more places than total solar eclipses.

_____ 10. You can always see the sun's corona.

MATCHING

Match each term in Column A with its description in Column B. Write the correct letter in the space provided.

Column A	Column B
_____ 1. umbra	a) sun's halo
_____ 2. penumbra	b) darker part of a shadow
_____ 3. solar eclipse	c) usually are not in a line
_____ 4. corona	d) sun blocked out
_____ 5. sun, earth, and moon	e) lighter part of a shadow

FILL IN THE BLANK

Complete each statement using a term or terms from the list below. Write your answers in the spaces provided. Some words may be used more than once.

solar eclipse	sun	total
earth	eclipse	darkness
partial	moves	moon
shadows	blocks	corona

1. A shadow is an area of _____ .

2. A shadow forms when an object _____ light.

3. The _____ and _____ block the sun's light. They

   cast long, cone-shaped _____ .

4. Sometimes the shadow of a heavenly body blocks out another heavenly body. This

   is called an _____ .

5. The blocking out of the sun by the moon's shadow is called a_____ .

6. A solar eclipse occurs when the _____ is between the

   _____ and the _____ .

7. When the moon blocks out all of the sun, we have a_____ solar

   eclipse.

8. When the moon blocks out a part of the sun, we have a _____

   solar eclipse.

9. During a total eclipse, we can see only the sun's rim. This is called the

   _____ .

10. The place where you can see a solar eclipse _____ across part of the

    earth's surface.

REACHING OUT

A solar eclipse can take place only during one moon phase. Which phase is it? Why?

_____

_____

SCIENCE *EXTRA*

Midnight 1991 — A Most Unusual Moment

Happy New Year! Midnight 1991 was very special. It marked an event that happens only once in a blue moon and the new year arrived one second late. Confused? Do not be. The explanations are interesting — and easy to understand.

You have learned about the moon phases. They range from a full moon to a new moon. The moon is full every 29 days, 12 hours, 44 minutes, and 29 seconds. But every month has 30 or 31 days, except for February, which has 28 days.

We see that each month has more time than it takes to complete one moon cycle. Therefore, in each month, a little bit of an additional phase is left over. These extra bits add up. As a result, sometimes, we have two full moons in one month. When this happens, the second full moon is called a blue moon. Why blue? No one knows.

A month with two full moons does not occur often — just once every two and a half years or so. This is where the term "once in a blue moon" comes from. "Once in a blue moon" means "not very often."

That explains why New Year's Eve marked an event that happens once in a blue moon, but why was it one second late?

Our system of time is based upon the rotation of the earth. It is based upon a constant rotation speed. That is where the problem arises! The earth's rotation speed is not constant.

On average, the earth's rotation is slowing. This deceleration is caused by friction, like the slowing of a spinning top. The tides of the oceans rub against the continents creating this friction. On average, the earth's rotation slows about 1/500 second each day. After 500 days, the earth's rotation has slowed by one second.

We now have ultra-accurate atomic clocks. So that the earth and these clocks are in sync, scientists add a second to the atomic clock. This added second is called a leap second.

The U.S. Naval Observatory in Washington D.C. is our nations timekeeper. There scientists like Brian Luzum and Dr. Dennis D. McCarthy, keep track of the earth's rotation. They decide if and when a leap second should be added. The first leap second was added in 1972. The seventeenth leap second was added on (you guessed it) December 31, 1990 just before midnight. Therefore, the new year arrived one second late.

What is a lunar eclipse? $\boxed{19}$

lunar eclipse: passing of the moon through the earth's shadow

LESSON 19 | What is a lunar eclipse?

As you know, the moon does not give off its own light. The moon gets its light from the sun. The light then reflects onto the earth.

The moon revolves around the earth. Most of the time the moon does not move into the earth's shadow. But sometimes it does. Since the earth is much bigger than the moon, the earth has a much bigger shadow. The moon can fit in this shadow. When the moon moves into the earth's shadow, we have a **lunar eclipse**.

During a lunar eclipse, hardly any sunlight reaches the moon. The moon becomes very dim.

You may ask, "How does the moon receive any sunlight when it is hidden in the earth's shadow?" The answer is that the earth's air "bends" some of the sun's light onto the moon. So, even when the moon is eclipsed, it is not completely blacked out. It just looks dull red.

A lunar eclipse lasts much longer than a solar eclipse. This is because the earth's shadow is very wide where the moon passes. The moon takes a long time to pass through.

From start to finish, a lunar eclipse lasts from three to four hours and sometimes longer.

A lunar eclipse can be seen from more areas of the earth than a solar eclipse. During a solar eclipse, the moon's shadow covers only a small part of the earth. A solar eclipse can be seen only on a small part of the earth. A lunar eclipse is different. During a lunar eclipse, the entire moon is in shadow. It can be seen from any part of the earth that is having night at the time of the eclipse.

Lunar eclipses happen more often than solar eclipses.

UNDERSTANDING A LUNAR ECLIPSE

Figure A shows a total lunar eclipse. Study it. Then fill in the blanks.

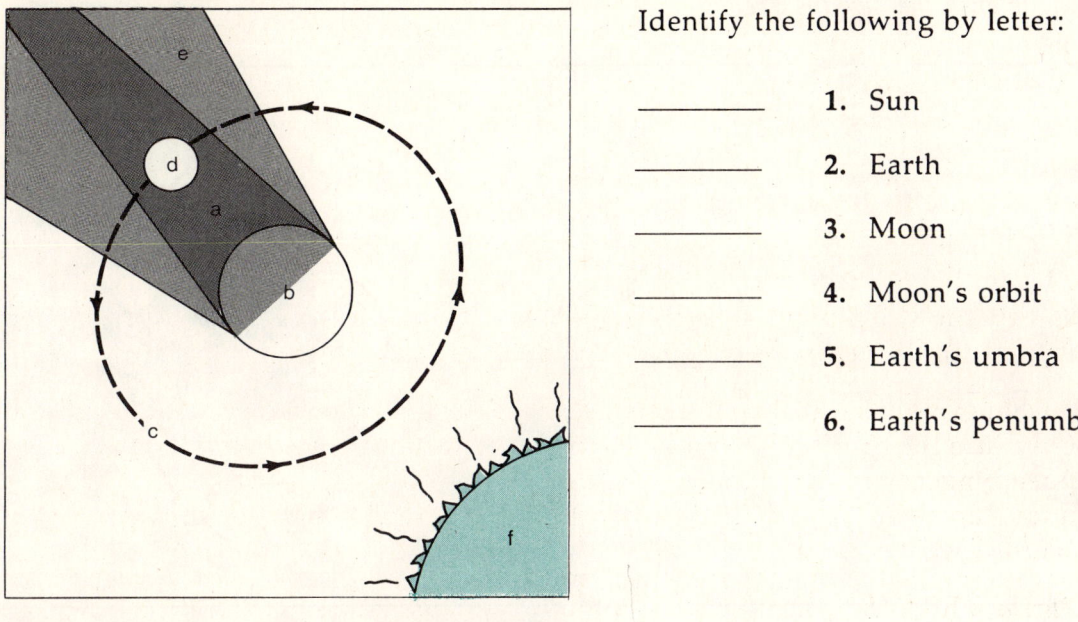

Identify the following by letter:

_____ 1. Sun

_____ 2. Earth

_____ 3. Moon

_____ 4. Moon's orbit

_____ 5. Earth's umbra

_____ 6. Earth's penumbra

Figure A   *During a lunar eclipse, the sun, earth and moon line up in a straight line with the earth in the middle.*

There are two kinds of lunar eclipses: <u>total</u> and <u>partial</u>.

The moon looks like this when it is not eclipsed:

A total lunar eclipse looks like this:

A partial lunar eclipse may look like any of these:

7. The moon is in total eclipse when it is in the earth's _____ .
   umbra, penumbra

8. The moon is in partial eclipse when it is in the earth's _____ .
   umbra, penumbra

9. When the moon is only partly in the earth's penumbra, the eclipse is

   _____ .
   total, partial

10. When the moon is partly in the umbra and partly in the penumbra, the eclipse is

    _____ .
    total, partial

Figure G shows the moon in five different positions. What does it look like in each position? Match the positions with the "moons" below.

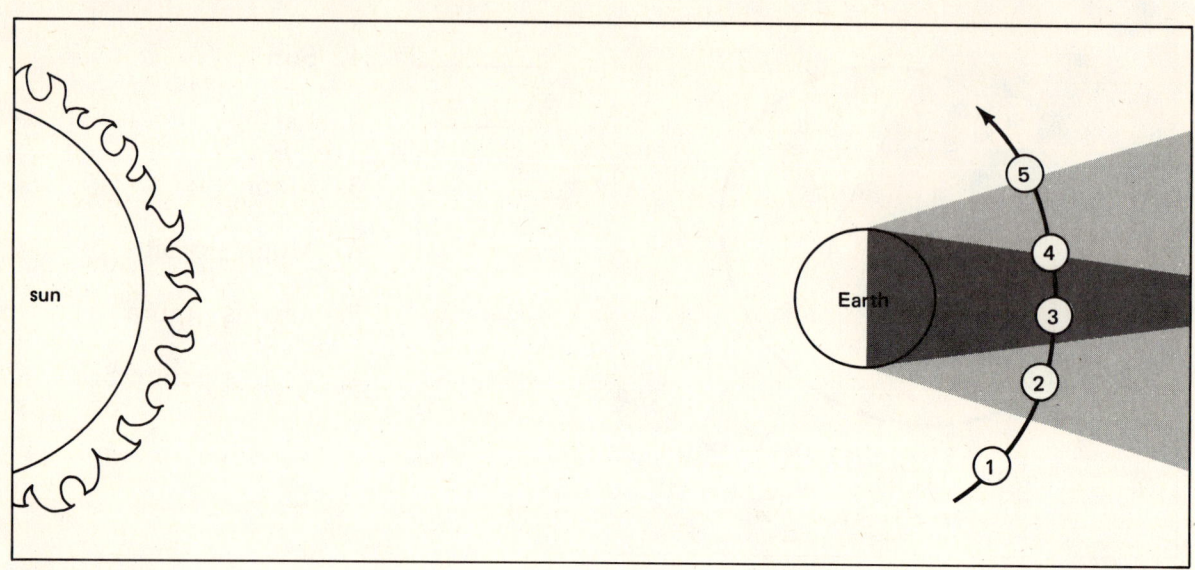

Figure B

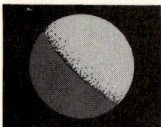

Figure C

Figure D

Figure E

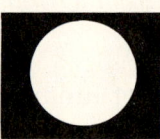

Figure F

Figure G

Answer by letter.

1. In position 1, the moon looks like _____ .

2. In position 2, the moon looks like _____ .

3. In position 3, the moon looks like _____ .

4. In position 4, the moon looks like _____ .

5. In position 5, the moon looks like _____ .

Now answer by number.

6. At which position is the moon not eclipsed at all?_____

7. Why is it not eclipsed? _____

8. At which position is the moon totally eclipsed? _____

9. At which positions is the moon partially eclipsed? _____ _____ _____

10. Which one is partially eclipsed the most? _____

TRUE OR FALSE

In the space provided, write "true" if the sentence is true. Write "false" if the sentence is false.

_____   **1.** The moon makes its own light.

_____   **2.** The moon reflects the sun's light.

_____   **3.** During a lunar eclipse, the moon is in the earth's shadow.

_____   **4.** During a lunar eclipse, part of the earth is in the moon's shadow.

_____   **5.** During a solar eclipse, part of the earth is in the moon's shadow.

_____   **6.** During a solar eclipse, the moon is in the earth's shadow.

_____   **7.** The whole moon can be covered by the earth's shadow.

_____   **8.** The whole earth can be covered by the moon's shadow.

_____   **9.** The darker part of a shadow is the umbra.

_____   **10.** The darker part of a shadow is the penumbra.

MATCHING

Match each term in Column A with its description in Column B. Write the correct letter in the space provided.

	Column A		Column B
_____	**1.** umbra	**a)**	lighter part of a shadow
_____	**2.** solar eclipse	**b)**	moon is in the earth's shadow
_____	**3.** lunar eclipse	**c)**	reflects the sun's light
_____	**4.** penumbra	**d)**	darker part of a shadow
_____	**5.** moon	**e)**	part of the earth is in the moon's shadow

FILL IN THE BLANK

Complete each statement using a term or terms from the list below. Write your answers in the spaces provided. Some words may be used more than once.

moon	dull red	earth
earth's atmosphere	does not	larger
predict	longer	disappear
reflects	sun	night

1. The moon _____ make its own light. The moon _____

   the sun's light.

2. During a lunar eclipse, the moon passes through the shadow of the

   _____ .

3. During a lunar eclipse, the _____ is between the _____

   and the _____ .

4. During a total lunar eclipse, the moon does not completely _____ .

5. A "totally" eclipsed moon is not completely blacked out because the

   _____ bends some light onto it.

6. An eclipsed moon looks _____ .

7. The earth's shadow is much _____ than the moon.

8. A lunar eclipse lasts _____ than a solar eclipse.

9. When a lunar eclipse is taking place, it can be seen from any part of the earth that

   is having _____ .

10. Scientists can _____ when and where eclipses will take place.

REACHING OUT

A lunar eclipse can take place only during one moon phase. Which phase is it? Why?

_____

_____

What causes tides?

20

high tide: time of high water level
low tide: time of low water level
neap [NEEP] **tide:**   tide that is not as high or low as normal tides
spring tide: tide that is higher and lower than normal tides
tide: daily change of the level of ocean water

LESSON 20 | What causes tides?

Have you ever spent a day at the beach? If you have, then you know that the water in the ocean does not stay at one level. At certain times of the day the water is higher than at other times. The water level rises and falls at regular time periods. We call this regular rise and fall of oceans **tides**.

There are **high tides** and **low tides**. Look at Figure A on the facing page. It shows a coastline at low tide. Figure B shows the same coastline at high tide—just a few hours later. Notice the difference in the water level.

Tides do not change suddenly. High tide moves in slowly. Then, after the water reaches its highest point, it moves out slowly. A low tide is followed by a high tide, which is followed by another low tide.

Most seashores have four tides every day—two high tides and two low tides. A change of tide takes about 6 hours and 12 minutes.

What causes tides?

Tides are caused by the pull of gravity by both the moon and the sun. The moon is more important because it is closer to the earth. The moon pulls on the earth with greater force than the sun.

The moon pulls upon the earth's land and water. The pull has hardly any effect upon the land. Rock does not move easily. But, water is different. Water moves <u>very</u> easily. It flows. The pull bulges the water on the part of the earth that is facing the moon. This part of the earth has high tide. There is also high tide on the opposite side of the earth—the side facing away from the moon.

Areas that supplied the water for high tide areas have low tides.

The earth is always rotating. As it turns, different parts face the moon. This causes the tides to keep changing.

Look at Figure A and B. Answer the questions.

Figure A *Low tide*

Figure B *High tide*

1. Why is the boat on land in Figure A? _____

2. About how long did the water take to change from Figure A to Figure B?

   _____

3. Which figure shows low tide? _____

4. Which figure shows high tide? _____

5. If you were a fisherman, at which tide would you unload your catch? _____

6. At which tide would you go to sea again? _____

7. How many times a day could you go to sea? _____

8. How many times a day could you unload your catch? _____

Study the figures. Then answer the questions.

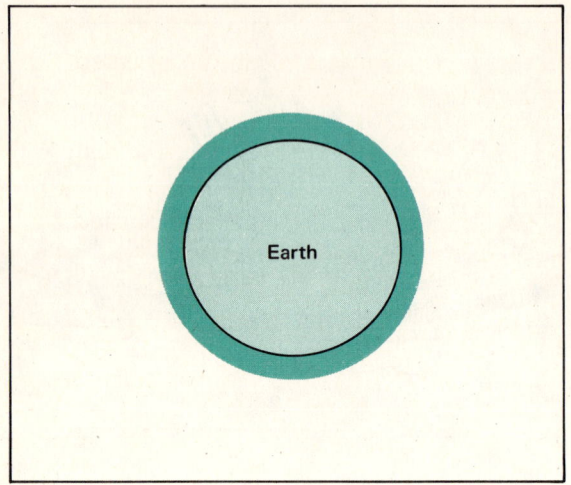

Figure C

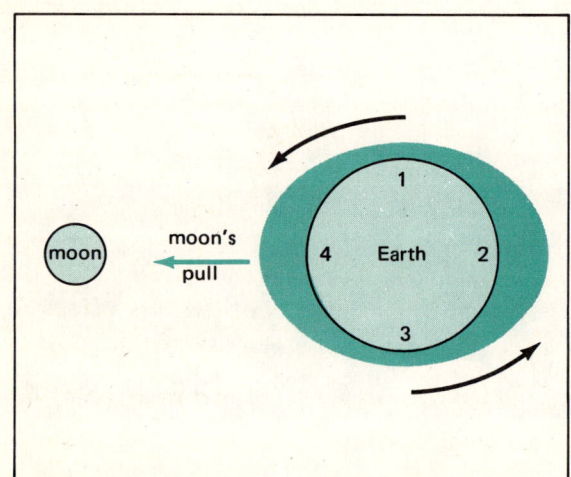

Figure D

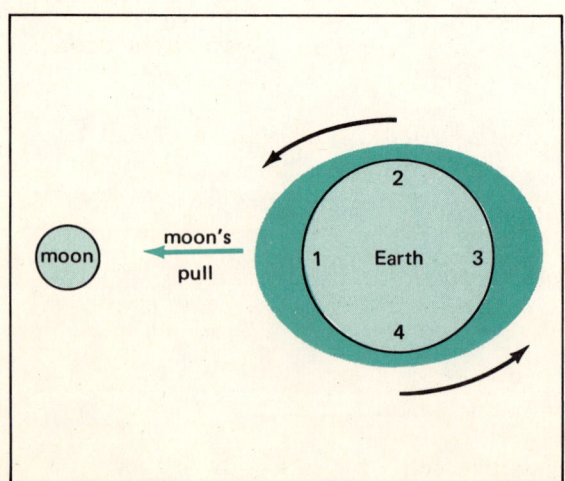

Figure E

If the moon and the sun did not pull on the earth, there would be no tides. The ocean level would be the same everywhere. However, the moon and the sun <u>do</u> pull on the earth.

1. Which one is more important in

    producing tides? _____
    sun, moon

2. Why? _____

    _____

3. Which side of the earth is facing

    the moon? _____
    1, 2, 3, 4

4. Which sides of the earth are

    having high tide? _____
    1, 2, 3, 4

5. Which sides are having low tide?

    _____
    1, 2, 3, 4

The earth rotates. As it rotates, different parts of the earth face the moon. The tides keep changing.

6. Which sides have high tide now?

    _____
    1, 2, 3, 4

7. Which sides have low tide?

    _____
    1, 2, 3, 4

8. About how much time has passed between Figures D and E?

    _____

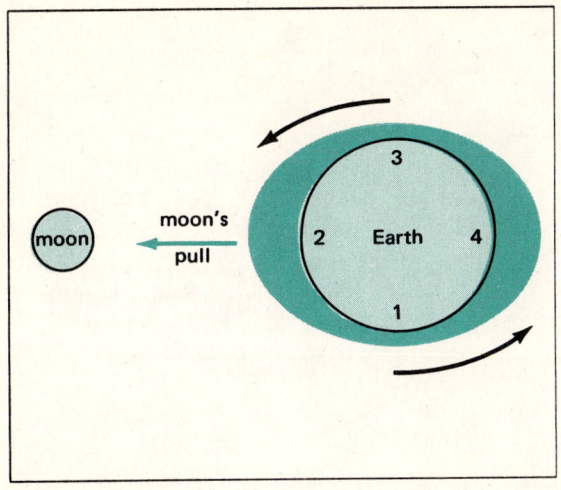

Figure F

9. Now, which sides have high tide?

   _____
   1, 2, 3, 4

10. About how much time has passed between Figures E and F?

    _____

11. About how much time has passed between Figures D and F?

    _____

12. How long before side 2 has high tide again? _____

13. Which other side will have high tide at the same time? _____

14. How long before side 3 has low tide again? _____

15. Which other side will have low tide at the same time? _____

TWO SPECIAL TIDES

The chief cause of tides is the moon. But the sun also has an effect on tides. Its effect is less. This is because the sun is so far away. Its pull upon the earth is very weak.

The sun's gravity helps produce two special kinds of tides: spring tides and neap [NEEP] tides.

- Spring tides happen twice a month—at new moon and at full moon. Spring tides produce high tides that are higher than usual. Spring tides produce low tides that are lower than usual.

- Neap tides happen twice a month also but at quarter moons. Neap tides produce moderate tides. That is, tides that are not as high and not as low as usual.

Do the following two exercises. They will help you understand spring and neap tides.

New moon

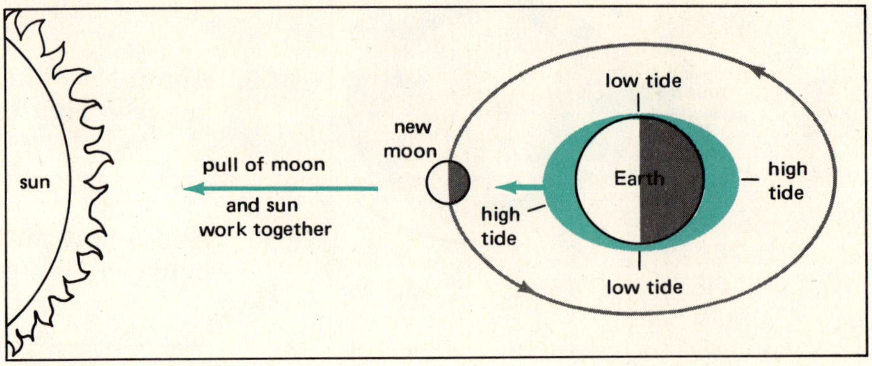

Figure G

*Full moon
(about 14 days later)*

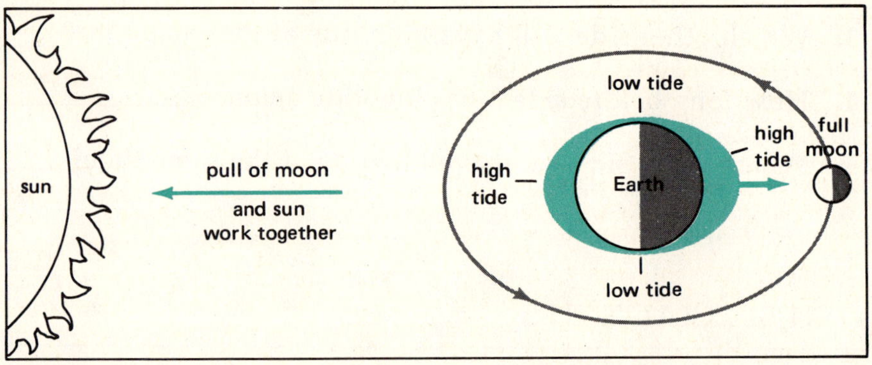

Figure H

1. At the new moon and at the full moon, the sun, earth, and moon

   _____ in a line.
   <small>are, are not</small>

2. When the sun, earth, and moon are in a line, the pull of gravity upon the earth

   becomes _____ .
   <small>stronger, weaker</small>

3. When the sun, earth, and moon are in a line, high tides are _____
   <small>higher, lower</small>

   than usual; low tides are _____ than usual.
   <small>higher, lower</small>

4. a) What do we call unusually high and low tides? _____

   b) How often do they happen? _____

5. At which moon phases do spring tides take place? _____ _____

First quarter moon

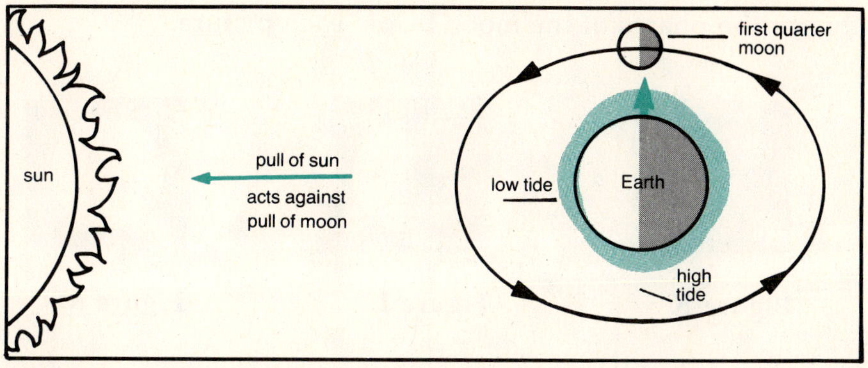

Figure I

Last quarter moon
(about 14 days later)

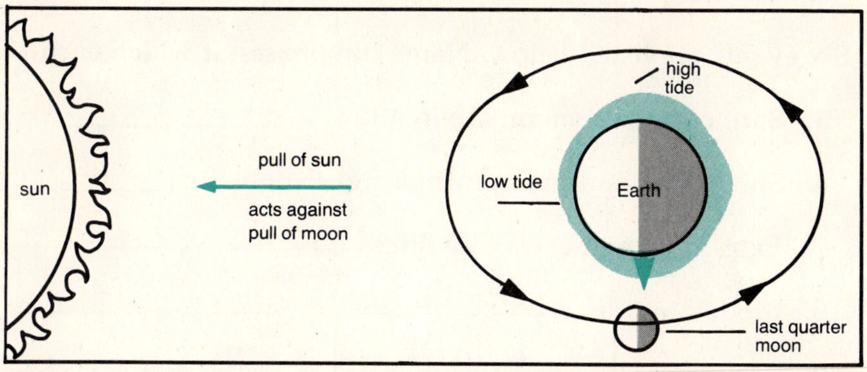

Figure J

6. At quarter moons, the sun, earth, and moon _____ in a line.
   are, are not

7. At quarter moons, the moon and sun are at right angles. Which of the following is

   a right angle? _____

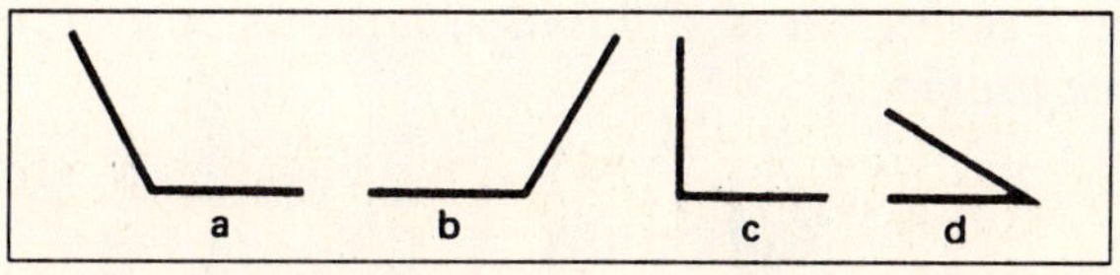

8. When the moon and sun are at right angles, the gravity pull upon the earth

   becomes _____ .
   stronger, weaker

9. When the moon and sun are at right angles, tides are _____ .
   extra high and extra low, not very high
   and not very low

10. Tides that are not very high and not very low are _____ tides.
    extreme, moderate

11. a) What do we call moderate tides? _____

    b) How often do they happen? _____

12. At which moon phases do neap tides take place? _____

WHICH PHASE?

Name the phases of the moon below each picture.

Figure K   **Figure L**   **Figure M**   **Figure N**

1. _____   2. _____   3. _____   4. _____

Six events are listed below. Name the phases at which each takes place.

5. Sun, earth and moon are in a line _____   _____

6. Sun, earth, and moon form a right angle _____   _____

7. Extra high and extra low tides _____   _____

8. Moderate tides _____   _____

9. Spring tides _____   _____

10. Neap tides _____   _____

MATCHING

Match each term in Column A with its description in Column B. Write the correct letter in the space provided.

Column A	Column B
_____ 1. spring tide	a) time of high water level
_____ 2. low tide	b) tide that is higher or lower than normal tides
_____ 3. gravity	c) force of attraction between objects
_____ 4. high tide	d) tide that is not as high or low as normal tides
_____ 5. neap tide	e) time of low water level

What is the solar system? | 21

asteroids [AST-uh-roydz]:   large chunks of rock that orbit the sun
meteoroid [MEE-tee-or-oyd]:   piece of rock or metal that orbits the sun
orbit: curved path of the one object around another object in space
satellite [SAT-uh-lite]:   natural or artificial object orbiting a body in space

LESSON 21 | What is the solar system?

Everywhere you look today, you see the word "solar". Solar energy. Solar power. What exactly does the word "solar" mean? "Solar" means "of, or relating to the sun."

The solar system, then, is the system of the SUN. This system is made up of the sun and all the objects that travel around the sun. These **satellites** [SAT-uh-lites] of the sun travel in "paths" called **orbits**. They are held in their orbits by the sun's gravity.

PLANETS Except for the sun itself, planets are the largest objects in the solar system. Nine planets orbit the sun. One of them is our own home, planet Earth.

MOONS Most planets have moons. Moons orbit the planets.

ASTEROIDS Asteroids [AST-uh-roydz] are large chunks of rock. Most asteroids are found in a "belt" between the planets Mars and Jupiter.

COMETS Comets are made up of rocks, dust and ice. A comet has a small "head" but a very long "tail." The tail extends millions of miles into space — and it points away from the sun. Comets travel around the sun in long elliptical orbits. The most famous comet is Halley's Comet. It takes Halley's Comet 76 years to complete one trip around the sun.

METEROIDS Meteroids [MEE-tee-or-oyds] are small bits of rock. Most are as small as a grain of sand. Some, however, are as large as boulders. Billions and billions of meteoroids are scattered throughout the solar system.

When a meteoroid enters the earth's atmosphere, friction causes the meteor to glow brightly. It seems to "burn up" as the rock changes it to a gas. While it is "burning up" it is called a meteor or a shooting star. We see it as a bright trail or streak of light in the night sky.

Most meteors burn up completely in the atmosphere. A few reach the earth's surface. A meteor that has reached the earth's surface is called a meteorite.

126

Study the figure. Then fill in the second column of the chart, listing the planets in order. Start with the planet closest to the sun.

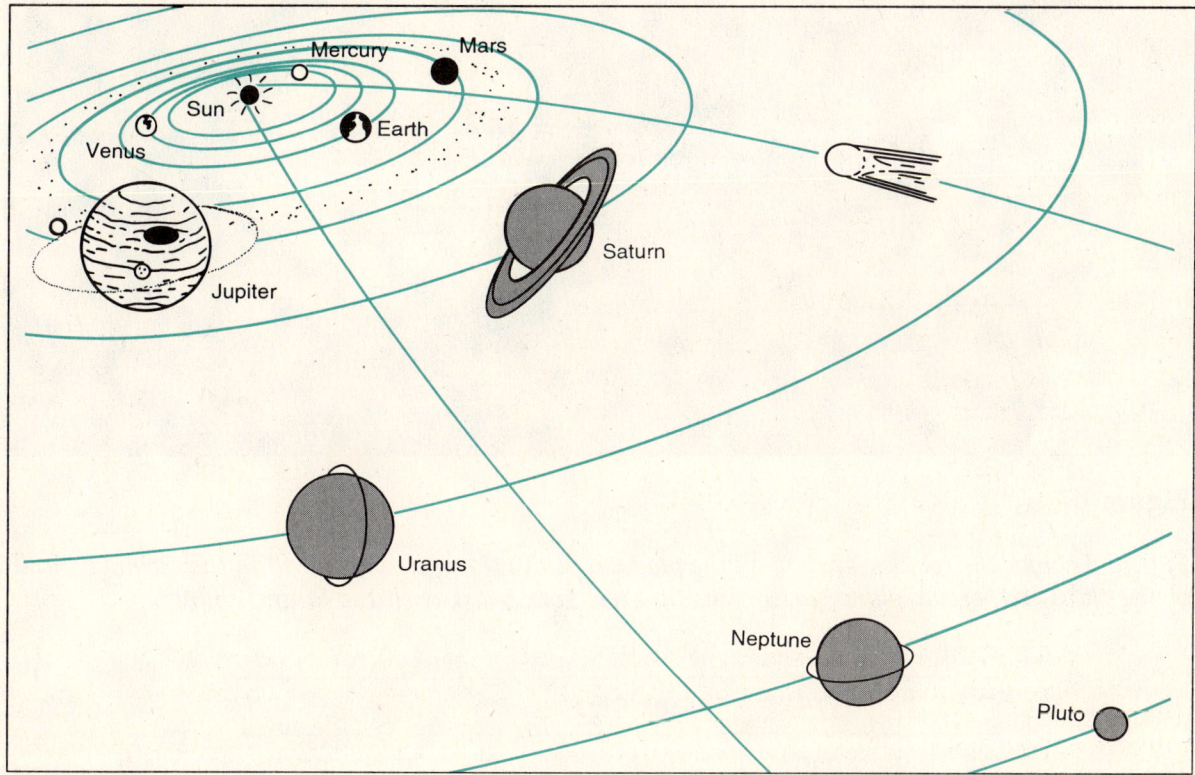

Figure A

Order of Planets from the Sun		
1.	(closest)	
2.		
3.		
4.		
5.		
6.		
7.		
8.		
9.	(farthest)	

Figure B

Figure B shows the relative sizes of all the planets. Study the figure. Then fill in the second column of the chart listing the planets according to their size. Start with the largest planet.

Planet Size		
1.	(largest)	
2.		
3.		
4.		
5.		
6.		
7.		
8.		
9.	(smallest)	

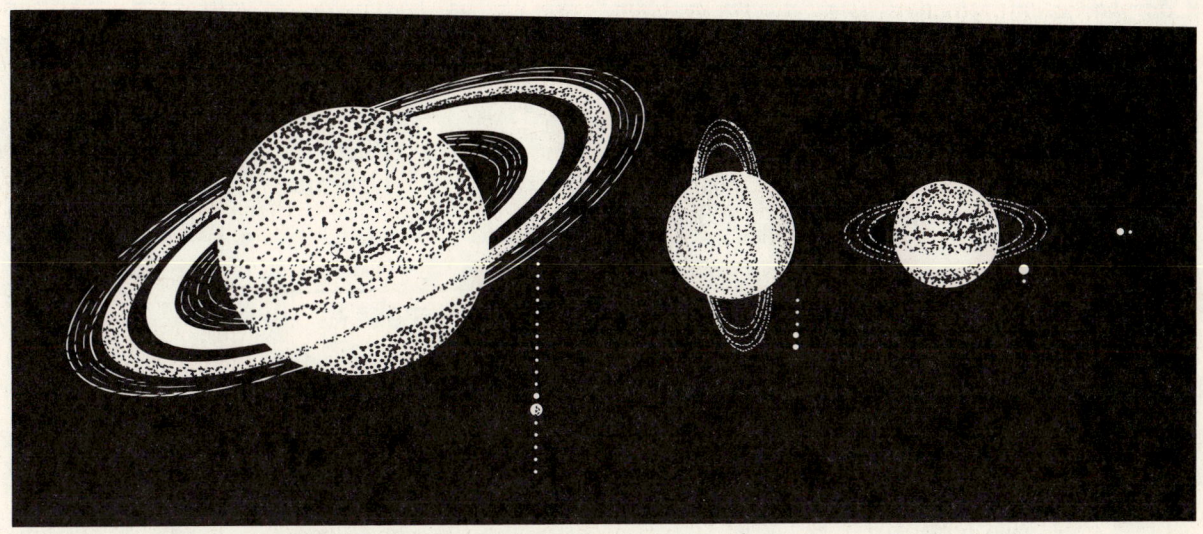

Use the figure to answer the following questions.

1. What do the white spheres near the planet stand for? _____

2. Only two planets have <u>no</u> moons. Name them. _____

   _____

3. Two planets have only <u>one</u> moon each. Name them. _____

   _____

4. Which planet has two moons? _____

5. Which two planets have the <u>most</u> moons? _____ _____

6. Which planets have <u>rings</u>? _____ _____

   _____ _____

7. The four planets closest to the sun are called the <u>inner planets</u>. Name the inner

   planets. _____ _____ _____

   _____

8. The five planets farthest from the sun are called the <u>outer planets</u>. Name the outer

   planets. _____ _____ _____

   _____ _____

FILL IN THE BLANK

Complete each statement using a term or terms from the list below. Write your answers in the spaces provided. Some words may be used more than once.

moons	comet	planets
Jupiter	solar system	Pluto
satellite	sun	Uranus
asteroids	Saturn	

1. The sun and all the space bodies that orbit the sun make up the

   _____ .

2. The largest objects that orbit the sun are called _____ .

3. The objects that orbit most <u>planets</u> are called _____ .

4. The rocks that form a "belt" between Mars and Jupiter are called

   _____ .

5. A _____ is made up of small bits of rock, dust, and ice.

6. A comet orbits the _____ .

7. The planets with rings are _____ , _____ , and

   _____ .

8. The largest planet is _____ .

9. The planet farthest from the sun is _____ .

10. Any space object that orbits another space object is called a _____ .

TRUE OR FALSE

In the space provided, write "true" if the sentence is true. Write "false" if the sentence is false.

_____ 1. The stars are part of our solar system.

_____ 2. The planets are satellites of the sun.

_____ 3. The Asteroid Belt is located between Mars and Jupiter.

_____ 4. Saturn is the only planet with rings.

_____ 5. All planets have moons.

What are the features of the sun?

chromosphere [KROH-muh-sfeer]:   layer of the sun's atmosphere above the photosphere
corona [kuh-ROH-nuh]:   outer layer of the sun's atmosphere
photosphere [FOH-tuh-sfeer]:   inner layer of the sun's atmosphere

LESSON 22 | What are the features of the sun?

The sun rises every morning, passes overhead, and sets every evening. The sun is part of our lives. What's more, the sun is essential to our lives. Without the sun there would be no life on earth.

The sun warms the earth. Without the sun the temperature of the earth would be several hundred degrees below zero. Plants get their energy from the sun. Animals get their energy from eating plants or eating animals that eat plants. Without the sun, all plants would soon die, and eventually, we would too.

We need the sun to survive. What do we know about the sun?

The sun is made up of gases only. It is much too hot for there to be solids or liquids. The sun is about three quarters hydrogen and about one quarter helium. There is a relatively tiny amount of other elements in the sun.

Like the earth, the sun is made up of several layers. They are:

CORE The core is the innermost and hottest layer of the sun. The temperature there is about 15 million degrees Celsius (27 million degrees Fahrenheit). The sun's energy is produced in the core.

RADIATION ZONE (4,500,000°C; 8,100,000°F) The radiation zone surounds the core. Solar energy (light) produced in the core moves outward through this section.

CONVECTION ZONE (1,100,000°C; 1,980,000°F) Huge streams of bubbling gases circulate in this layer of the sun. This circulation transfers the heat generated inside the sun at the sun's surface.

PHOTOSPHERE (5,700°C; 10,300°F) The glowing gases in the photosphere [FOH-tuh-sfeer] light the solar system. The photosphere is the part of the sun we see.

The sun is very very bright. Unless you have very special filters, you should never look directly at the sun. Looking at the sun can cause permanent eye damage, even blindness.

There are other ways to study the sun, SO DON'T DO IT!

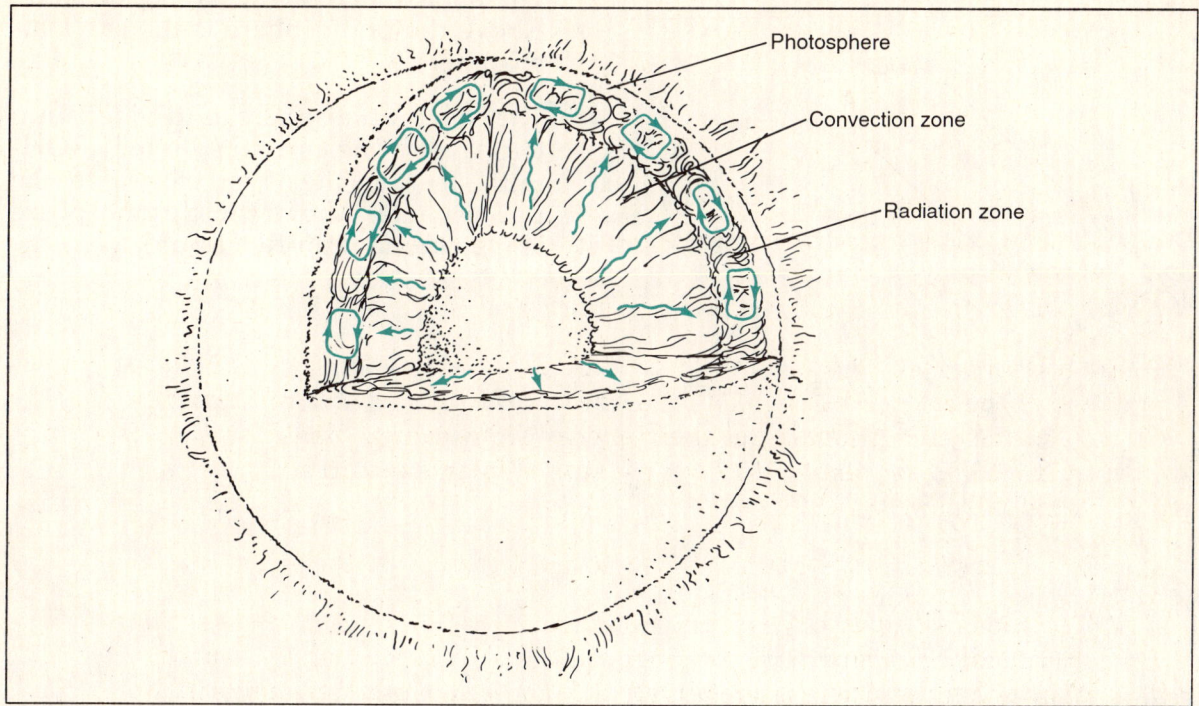

Figure A   *The layers of the sun*

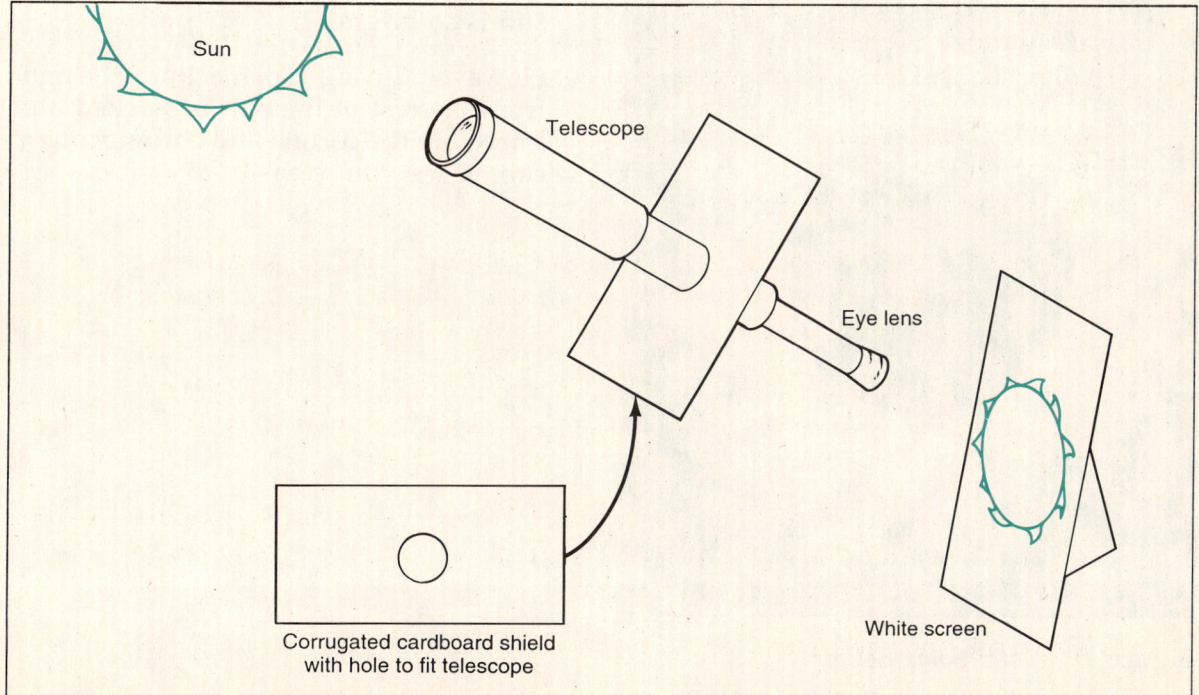

Figure B   *How to study the sun safely*

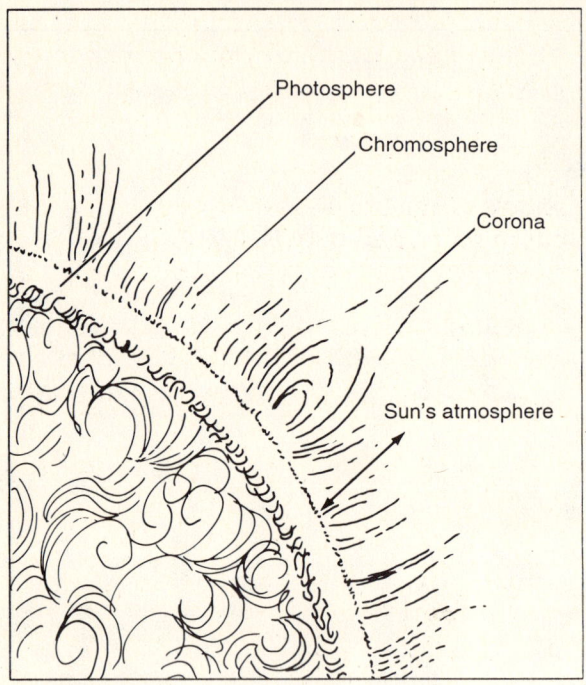

Figure C

The photosphere is the sun's "surface." Above the photosphere is the sun's atmosphere.

The sun's atmosphere is divided into two layers. The **chromosphere** [KROH-muh-sfeer] is the layer closest to the photosphere. Above the chromosphere is the **corona** [kuh-ROH-nuh].

Figure D *Total Solar Eclipse*

The chromosphere and corona usually cannot be seen from earth because the sun is so bright.

However, during a solar eclipse, the light from the rest of the sun is blocked out. Therefore the corona and chromosphere can be seen quite easily.

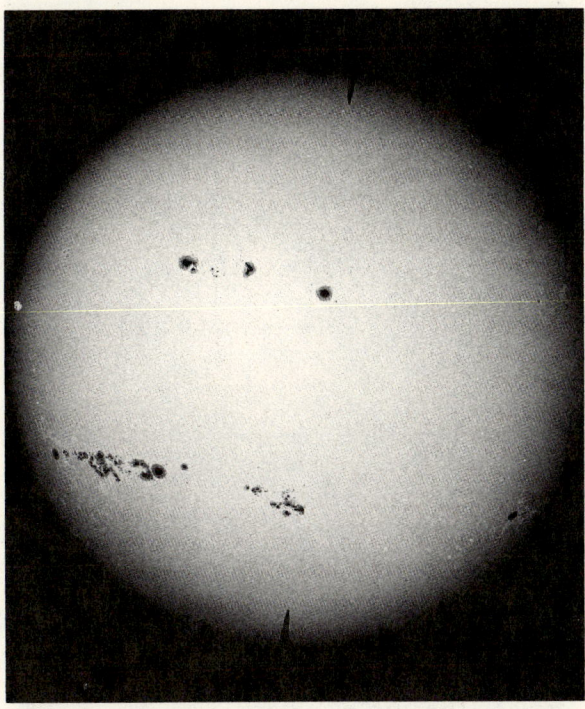

Figure E *Sunspots*

Sunspots are dark patches of gases in the photosphere. They look dark because they are "cooler" than the gases around them. But they are still very hot — about 3,500°C.

Sunspots are magnetic "storms" and have strong magnetic fields. They usually occur in pairs, and may last from a few days to several weeks before disappearing.

The number of sunspots increase and then decrease in a regular pattern. This is called the sunspot cycle. One sunspot cycle takes about 11 years.

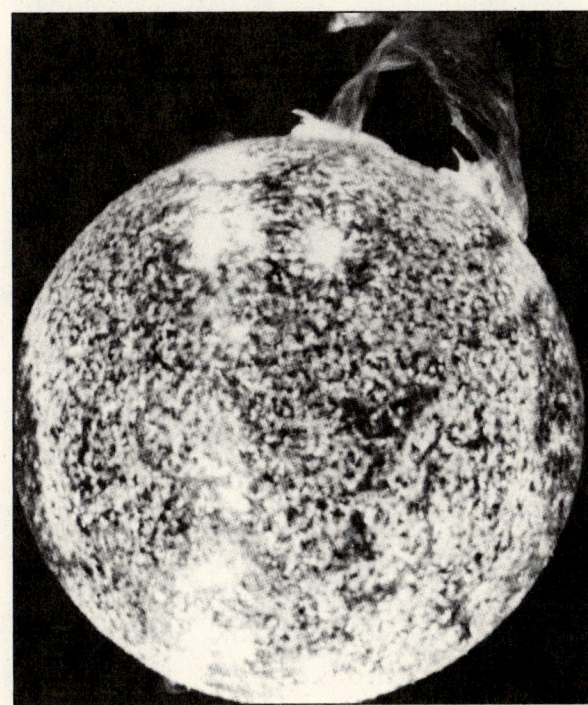

Figure F *Solar Flare*

Sometimes, at the peak of a sunspot cycle, tremendous explosions of solar gases take place near sunspots. The eruption of these gases out of the photosphere are called solar flares.

Solar flares shoot atomic particles and radiation into space. Some reach the earth's atmosphere. They interfere with radio communications. Solar flares even affect the weather.

FILL IN THE BLANK

Complete each statement using a term or terms from the list below. Write your answers in the spaces provided.

blindness	photosphere	permanent	gases
chromosphere	sunspots	convection zone	core
radiation zone	weather	total solar eclipse	energy
radio communication	layers	see	corona

1. Looking directly at the sun can cause _____ eye damage and even _____ .

2. The sun is divided into _____ of _____ .

3. The innermost section of the sun is the _____ . This is where the sun produces its _____ .

4. Solar energy is transferred outward from the core through the _____.

5. The _____ transfer solar energy to the sun's surface.

6. The sun's surface is called the _____ . This is the layer we can _____ .

7. The layers of the sun's atmosphere are the _____ , and the _____ .

8. The chromosphere and the corona can be seen with the unaided eye only during a _____ .

9. Patches of less hot gases in the photosphere are called _____ .

10. Sunspots affect _____ and _____ .

REACHING OUT

Suppose the number of sunspots was low in 1988. When will the next period of low sunspot activity occur? Why? _____

_____

_____

What are the inner planets?

23

inner planets: the four planets closest to the sun
terrestrial [tuh-RES-tree-uhl] **planets:** planets that are similar to Earth in their size and composition

LESSON 23 | What are the inner planets?

The four planets closest to the sun are called the **inner planets.** The inner planets are similar in a number of ways. The inner planets are also called the **terrestrial** [tuh-RES-tree-uhl] **planets**. Terrestrial means "like the Earth."

The terrestrial plants are relatively small compared to the other planets in the solar system. Unlike the outer planets, they have very little hydrogen and helium. Instead, they are made mostly of rock and iron.

Everything in the solar system formed out of the same mixture of interstellar matter. This interstellar matter was mostly hydrogen and helium. What happened to the hydrogen and helium on the inner planets?

Scientists believe it simply blew away. The inner planets are much smaller than the outer planets. Therefore, the pull of gravity on the inner planets is much smaller. Hydrogen and helium are very light. It takes a strong pull to keep them around a planet. The inner planets did not have a strong enough pull.

Instead, the hydrogen and helium floated out into space. There, particles being shot off from the sun pushed the hydrogen and helium out of the solar system.

Figure A

Mercury is the planet closest to the sun. It is about one third the size of earth and is only one twentieth as massive.

Mercury has no moons and is very similar to Earth's moon. Like the Moon, Mercury has virtually no atmosphere and is heavily cratered.

Mercury rotates on its axis once every 59 days. Since it is closer to the sun than any of the other planets, Mercury takes less time to go around the sun than any other planet. It only takes Mercury 88 days to go all the way around the sun.

The rate of rotation and revolution on Mercury act together to give every place on Mercury 88 days of daylight followed by 88 days of darkness. This causes huge differences in daytime and nighttime temperatures on Mercury. The temperature on Mercury during the day is about 400 degrees Celsius (750°F). At night, the temperature is about 180 degrees below zero Celsius (-290°F). That's quite a change!

The *Mariner 10* spacecraft flew past Mercury three times in 1974 and 1975. This is the only spacecraft to ever visit Mercury. Figure A shows a picture of the planet which was made by putting many detailed photos together.

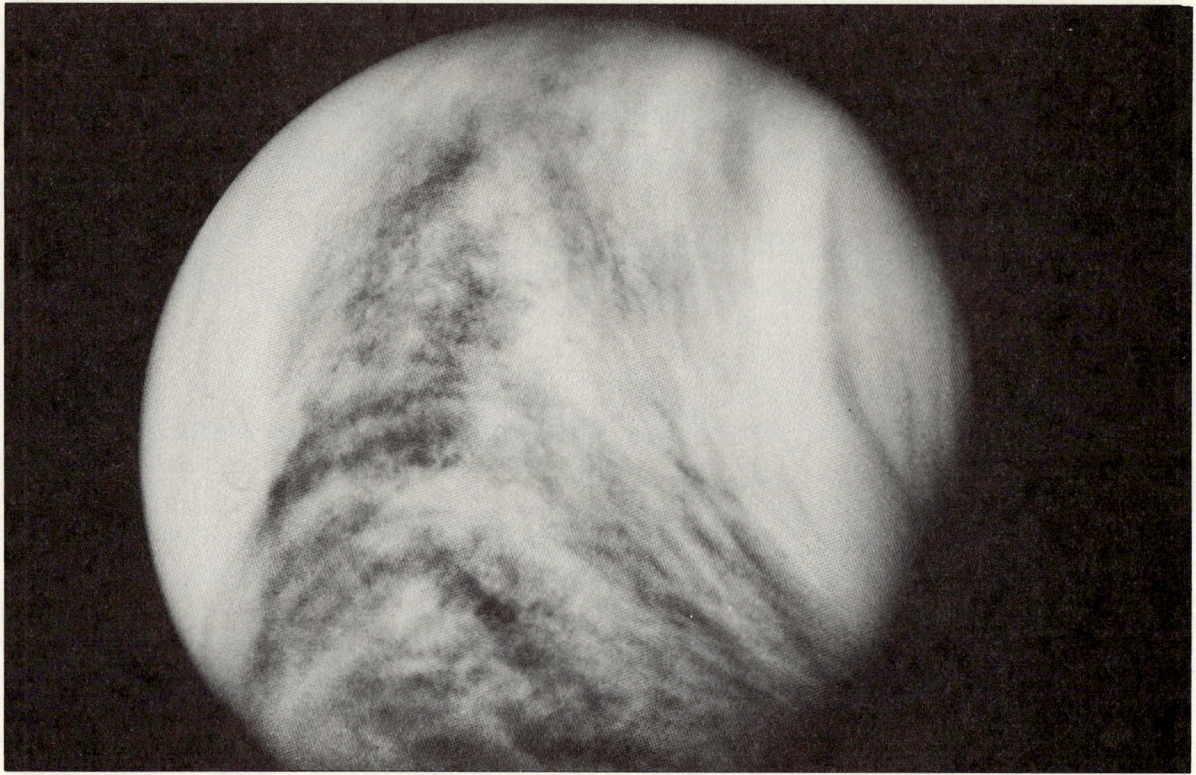

Figure B

Venus has nearly the same size and mass as Earth. It is often referred to as Earth's sister world.

Venus takes 225 days to go around the sun. Venus rotates very slowly and in the opposite direction of most of the other planets. Scientists believe that Venus once rotated at the same rate that it revolved around the sun, once every 225 days. It always had the same side towards the sun. Earth, however, pulls on Venus as well and Venus now spins so that when it is closest to Earth, it always has the same side facing Earth.

Venus is closer to the sun. If you guessed that Venus is warmer than the earth, you would be right. But the fact that Venus is closer to the sun is only part of the reason that it is so warm. The atmosphere of Venus has a lot of carbon dioxide in it. Carbon dioxide acts like a one way door. The carbon dioxide lets the warmth of the sun reach the surface of Venus very easily. It does not, however, let that heat escape into space very easily. Instead, Venus has gotten warmer and warmer, like you do under a blanket. The temperature on Venus is about 480 degrees Celsius (900°F).

Furthermore, Venus's atmosphere is so thick that the spacecraft that have orbited it have not been able to photograph the surface. Instead, radar is used to map the surface. *Magellan* is a radar mapping space probe that is currently mapping the surface.

Figure C

Earth is your home. It is the home of your family, the home of your friends, the home of everyone you know. Only a few people (astronauts and cosmonauts) have ever left Earth.

We do not usually think of Earth as a planet. It's kind of like not seeing a forest because of the trees. We are so close to Earth (it's right beneath our feet) that we do not recognize it as a planet. It is a planet, and as our home world, it is very important to us.

Earth is the only planet in the solar system we know that has living things on it. There are several reasons why this is so.

The temperatures on Earth are just right for living things to have formed several million years ago, and for living things to survive today.

The temperature on Earth is important for another reason. Water is a liquid on Earth. On planets closer to the sun, the temperatures are higher than Earth's and water is found only as a gas. On planets farther away from the sun than Earth, it is colder and water is found only as a solid.

On Earth, however, we have oceans of liquid water, and liquid water is needed by living things. The next time you go outside, consider how lucky you are to have Earth for your home.

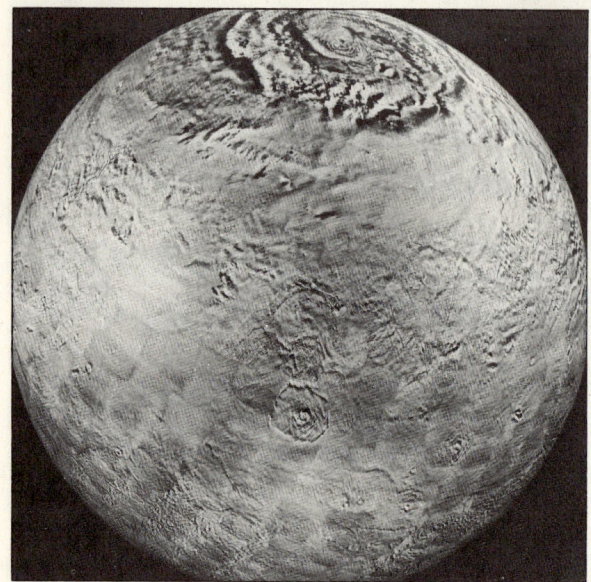

Figure D   **Figure E**

Mars is about half the size of Earth and is twice the size of the moon. A red dust covers the planet and you can recognize Mars in the sky because of its reddish color.

People have often wondered about Mars. In 1877, an Italian astronomer named Giovanni Schiaparelli noticed dark markings he called canali, which means "channels." The American astronomer Percival Lowell interpreted Shiaparelli's writings to mean that Mars had canals like the canals on Earth. Lowell thought that these canals must have been created by Martians, intelligent beings on Mars. For half a century, people would imagine little green men and women lived on Mars.

In fact, when a fictional story about an invasion from Mars was broadcast on the radio in the 1930s, many people thought it was real!

We now know that there are no little green men and women on Mars, but the possibility that there could be life still exists. Water is a necessary ingredient in the development of life on a planet, and Mars once had a great deal of water. Even though the planet is now very dry, if there had been life on Mars when the planet had more water, the life forms could have evolved to live in the present dry climate.

In 1976, two *Viking* spacecraft landed on Mars. One of their main objectives was to check the Martian surface for life. They found many of the necessary ingredients for life but no evidence that there was actually anything alive on the planet.

FILL IN THE BLANK

Complete each statement using a term or terms from the list below. Write your answers in the spaces provided. Some words may be used more than once.

Mercury	Earth	liquid
Venus	Mars	*Viking* spacecraft
terrestrial	*Mariner 10*	moon

1. _____ is the planet closest to the sun.

2. Mercury is similar to Earth's_____ .

3. Mercury, Venus, Earth and Mars are _____ planets.

4. _____ and _____ are about the same size.

5. _____ was a spacecraft that studied Mercury.

6. _____ has a very thick atmosphere.

7. _____ is the only planet known to have life on it.

8. On Earth, water is usually found as a _____ .

9. _____ is a red planet.

10. In 1975, two _____ landed on _____ .

MATCHING

Match each term in Column A with its description in Column B. Write the correct letter in the space provided.

Column A

_____ 1. *Magellan*

_____ 2. *Viking*

_____ 3. *Mariner 10*

_____ 4. Venus

_____ 5. Mars

Column B

a) half the size of Earth

b) studied Mars

c) studying Venus

d) studied Mercury

e) same size as Earth

CROSSWORD PUZZLE

Use the clues to complete the crossword puzzle.

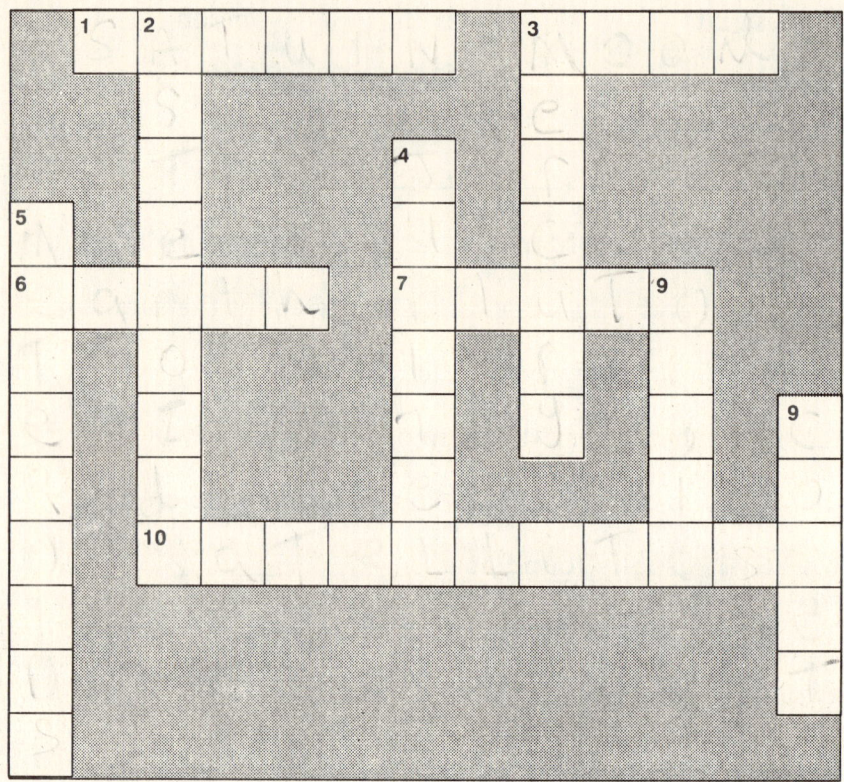

Clues

Across

1. First planet known to have rings
3. Body that orbits a planet
6. The planet we live on
7. Farthest planet from the sun
10. The sun and everything that travels around it

Down

2. Found in a belt between Mars and Jupiter
3. Planet nearest to the sun
4. Largest planet
5. "Shooting star"
8. "Paths" in which objects travel around the sun
9. Travels in long, cigar-shaped path around the sun

What are the outer planets?

24

gas giants: planets that are large and primarily composed of gases

LESSON 24 | What are the outer planets?

Beyond the orbit of Mars lies an asteroid belt that mark the boundary between the inner planets and the outer planets. The inner planets are generally the same size and made of the same rocky material.

In general, the outer planets are totally different from the inner planets.

Jupiter, Saturn, Uranus, and Neptune are gas giants. The smallest of the four, Neptune, is 60 times the size of Earth. As their name suggests, gas giants are primarily made of gases. They are very similar to stars that never started shining. In fact, some scientists suggest that if Jupiter had been a few times larger, it would have become a star.

The one outer planet that is not a gas giant is Pluto, the small planet that belongs in a class by itself.

Figure A *Jupiter, Io, and Europa*

Jupiter, like the other planets, is named after a mythological Roman god. The mythological Jupiter was king of the gods and Jupiter is king of the planets. Jupiter is the largest planet in the solar system.

The most prominent feature of Jupiter is its red spot. This storm in its atmosphere has been raging for as long as we have been able to see it. With the exception of the red spot, Jupiter's atmosphere can be described as a number of bands stretching around the planet.

Jupiter has four very large moons that can be seen with even the weakest telescopes. These moons, discovered by Galileo, are called the Galilean satellites. The giant planet also has about a dozen smaller moons.

Io, the smallest moon, is a fiery world with very active volcanos, caused by Jupiter's gravitational pull on the moon. Europa is an extremely smooth moon which has an icy surface. Caliosto and Ganymede are two moons about the size of Mercury. Calisto is very similar to Mercury and Earth's moon in that it is covered with craters. Ganymede is not completely understood since it is largely made of ice. From a geological perspective, ice is a very complex material.

Almost all we know about Jupiter was learned by the *Voyager 1* and *Voyager 2* flybys. These two spacecraft took a tour of the outer solar system in the 1970s and 1980s and Jupiter was the first planet they encountered. The cameras on the *Voyager* spacecraft took pictures far, far better than any that could be taken from Earth. The spacecraft also carried other equipment which performed a number of other experiments as the spacecraft flew past Jupiter.

One of the most important discoveries made by Voyager spacecraft was that Jupiter has a ring around it. This ring is much fainter than the one around Saturn or Neptune. The discovery of a ring around Jupiter showed that most gas giants in the solar system have rings.

Figure B

Saturn is known as the ringed planet. From Earth, it is relatively easy to see four distinct rings through a telescope. When *Voyager* reached Saturn, however, no one was prepared for what it found. There were thousands of rings! Almost too many to count. The rings are made of dust and rocks of various sizes.

Voyager 1 flew past Jupiter in March, 1979. The gravity of Jupiter then catapulted it towards Saturn, which it reached in November 1980. This push allowed *Voyager 1* to reach Saturn much more quickly using far less energy. *Voyager 2* was pushed by Jupiter in the same manner. What's more, Saturn's gravitational pull pushed *Voyager 2* on to Uranus. Uranus in turn, pushed *Voyager 2* on towards Neptune.

Scientists were able to plot this course for th*e Voyage*r spacecraft because the planets were on a special alignment. This alignment only happens about once every two hundred years.

Saturn has a large number of moons. Titan, the largest of these moons is bigger than the planet Mercury. Titan is both larger and colder than Earth's moon. Titan's temperature and mass allow it to have a thick atmosphere. In fact, it has more of an atmosphere than Mars or Earth. Like Earth, Titan's atmosphere is mostly made up of nitrogen. The conditions on Titan are very similar to what existed on Earth a long time ago, with one important exception. Titan is much colder than Earth. The temperature on Titan is 177 degrees below zero Celsius (-180°F). Still, studying Titan may help us understand the Earth's own history.

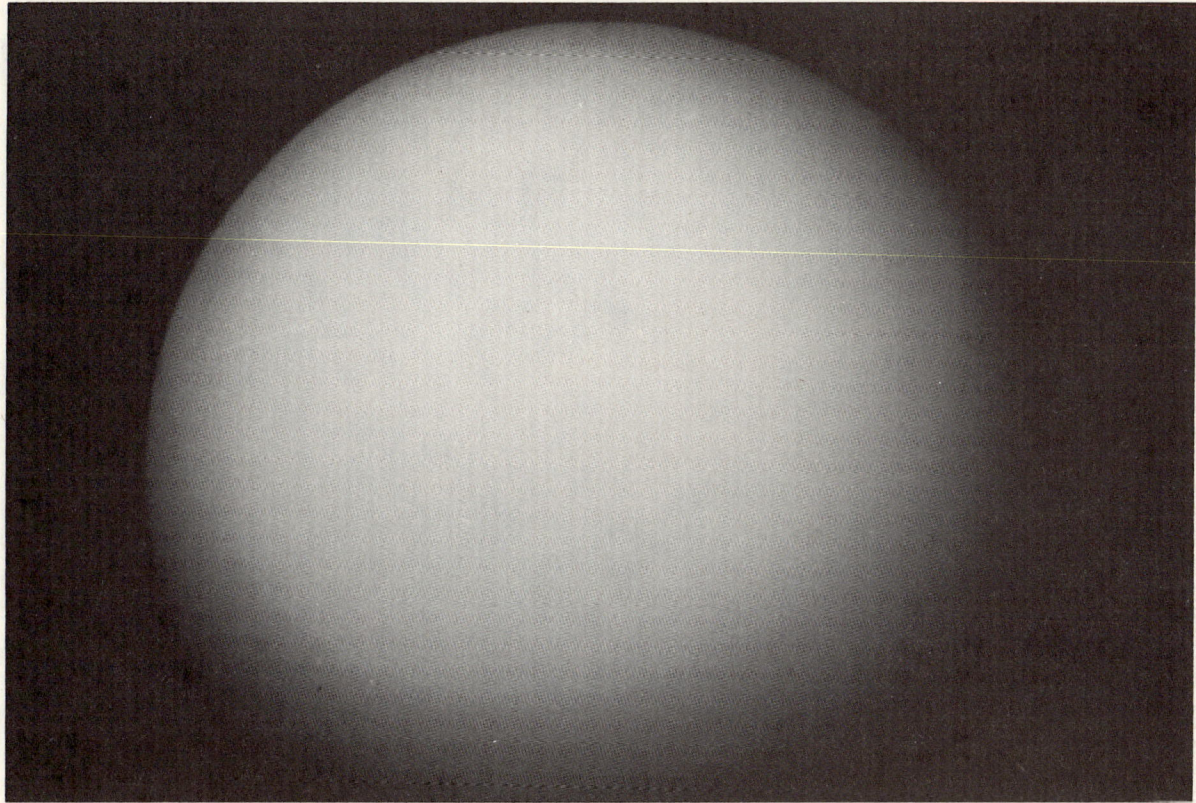

Figure C

For many years, Uranus and Neptune have been thought of as twins. Both planets are roughly the same size, with a diameter of about 50,000 kilometers. They both also have a deep blue color, like the sky on a very clear day. However, as we have learned more about these two worlds, some differences have been discovered between these two brothers.

Uranus was discovered in 1781. Five years after the United States had declared independence from Britain, an amateur astronomer named William Herschel was using a six inch telescope to study some stars. One of the stars appeared as a disk on his telescope rather than a point of light. He watched it over a period of many nights and discovered it moved with respect to the other stars. What Hershel had discovered was not a star but was a planet, what we now call the planet Uranus.

On March 10, 1977, Jim Elliot, a professional astronomer, studied Uranus as it passed in front of a bright star. Astronomers can tell a lot about a planet by watching it eclipse a star. The light from the star was blocked as the planet passed in front of the star. Furthermore, the light was blocked out just before and just after it passed by the planet. The cause of this was a set of rings that were too small to be seen from Earth. Until this discovery, Saturn was the only planet we knew that had rings. Now we know that several planets have them.

When *Voyager* 2 visited Uranus, its cameras showed that the atmosphere of the planet is very smooth, unlike the storms and bands visible in the other gas giants.

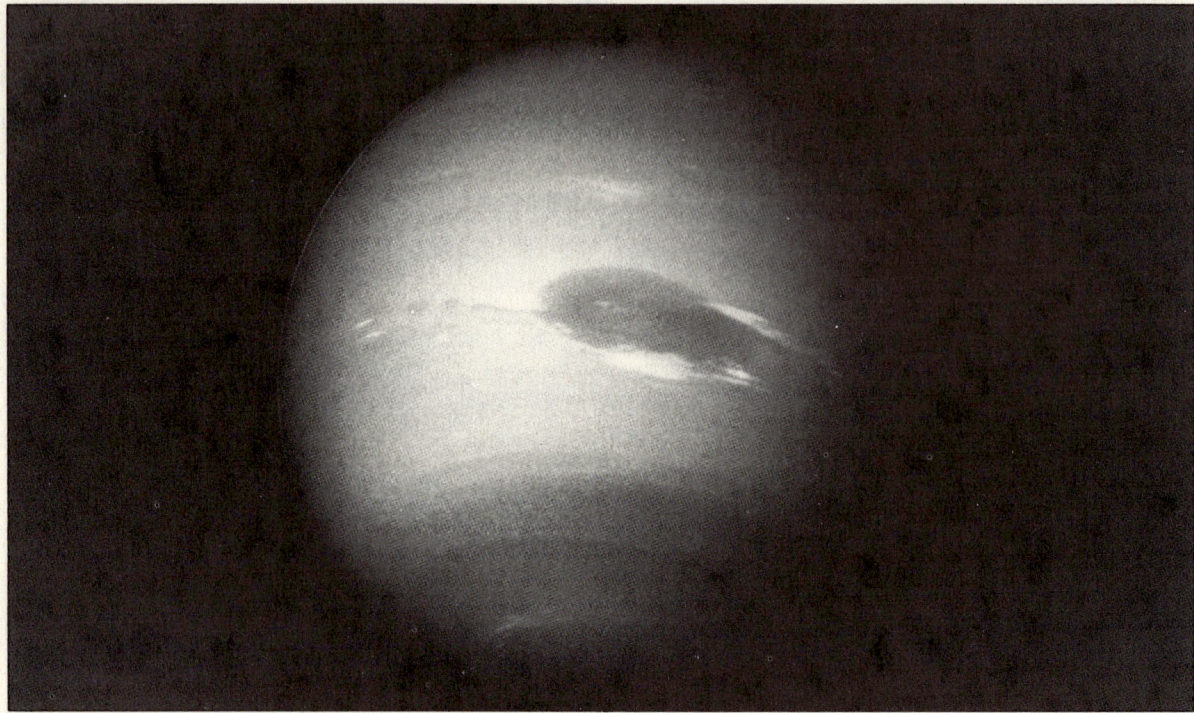

Figure D

Once Uranus had been discovered, astronomers rushed to plot and calculate its orbit around the sun. They could not figure it out. Even after calculating the effect of all the other planets on Uranus, it still did not follow the predicted orbit. Scientists suggested that there must be another planet farther out than Uranus that had not been discovered. They then set out to calculate where it would be. A search was made.

On September 23, 1846 Neptune was discovered almost exactly where John Couch Adams and Urbain Jean Joseph LeVerrier, two mathematicians, had predicted it would be found. This was a tremendous triumph for science and mathematics.

While Neptune resembles Uranus in its color, its atmosphere resembles Jupiter's atmosphere. Instead of a large red spot, Neptune has a large dark spot.

After rings were discovered on Uranus and Jupiter, scientists wondered if Neptune had rings. A search for rings around Neptune was undertaken. The same process that found the rings around Uranus was used, but was not effective. Scientists would sometimes find the light blocks on one but not the other. Since rings go around both sides of the planet, they should block the light on both sides

Voyager 2 solved the controversy by clearly showing that Neptune had rings. An individual ring was sometimes thicker on one side than it was on the other. Scientists on Earth could only detect the thicker part of the rings.

In 1610, Galileo first saw the rings around Saturn. For the next 367 years, people believed that Saturn was the only planet that had a ring system. In thirteen years, from 1977 to 1990, scientists have learned that all the gas giants have rings. That is an amazing discovery in such a short period of time.

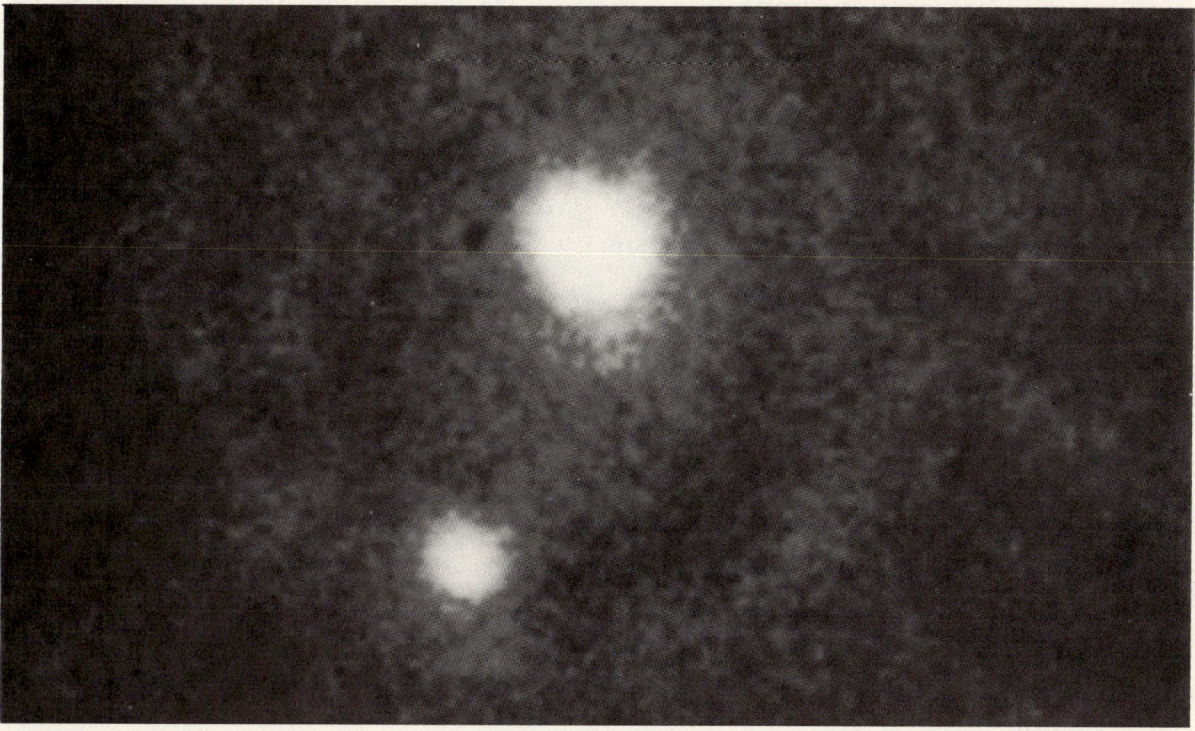

Figure E

After the discovery of Neptune astronomers continually wondered whether there could be a ninth planet. Sometimes, searches were made for such an object. One search was carried out at Lowell observatory, founded by the same Percival Lowell who thought there were canals on Mars. Clyde Tombaugh, an assistant at the observatory, would study two pictures of the same section of the sky taken at different times. He would look to see whether any object in the picture had moved. On February 18, 1930, Tombaugh discovered Pluto.

Pluto usually is the farthest planet from the sun. Its orbit is very elliptical and it crosses the orbit of Neptune. Right now it is closer to the sun than Neptune and it will be until 1999.

We do not know very much about Pluto since it is so far away and no spacecraft have visited it. Pluto is the smallest planet in the solar system and is slightly smaller than the Moon. It has a moon of its own named Charon and a very thin atmosphere made mostly of methane.

Since it is so far from the sun, Pluto is very cold. It usually is about 225° below zero Celsius (-373°F) on Pluto.

Some scientists do not think that Pluto should be considered a planet. It is very different than all the other planets in the solar system. It is most like some of the moons of the gas giants.

Unfortunately, there are no plans to send a spacecraft to Pluto, even though it is the only planet that has not yet been visited. For the time being, at least, much about Pluto will remain a mystery.

FILL IN THE BLANK

Complete each statement using a term or terms from the list below. Write your answers in the spaces provided. Some words may be used more than once.

Voyager 1	Jupiter	Neptune	gas giants
Voyager 2	Saturn	Uranus	Pluto

1. _____ is the largest planet.

2. The first planet known to have rings was _____ .

3. _____ and _____ are bluish in color.

4. Neptune, Uranus, Jupiter and Saturn are _____ .

5. _____ is the farthest planet from the sun right now.

6. _____ is usually the farthest planet from the sun.

7. _____ and _____ are spacecraft that flew by

Jupiter and Saturn.

8. _____ also flew by Uranus and Neptune.

9. _____ is the smallest planet.

10. _____ was not visited by *Voyager 1* or *Voyager 2*.

MATCHING

Match each term in Column A with its description in Column B. Write the correct letter in the space provided.

	Column A	Column B
_____	1. Io	a) moon of Pluto
_____	2. Charon	b) moon of Saturn
_____	3. Titan	c) volcanic moon of Jupiter
_____	4. Triton	d) four Galilean moons
_____	5. Ganymede, Calisto, Europa, and Io	e) moon of Neptune

What are stars?

absolute [AB-suh-loot] **magnitude:**   true brightness of a star
apparent [uh-PER-unt] **magnitude:**   brightness a star seems to have
magnitude [MAG-nuh-tood]:   star brightness

LESSON 25 | What are stars?

Our sun is a star. In fact, our sun is a very average star. There are billions and billions of stars in the galaxy. Some are as bright as the sun. Some are much, much brighter. Why, then, does the sun appear to be so much larger and brighter than all the other stars? Because it is so much closer to Earth than the next nearest star. The sun's brightness is apparent brightness!

If something is hot enough, it will "glow." It will give off light. Stars are made up of very hot gases. "Starlight"—the light given off by stars—is the light given off by the very hot gases that make up the stars.

Without a telescope, stars look like tiny points of white light. Actually, light from different stars can be different in two important ways—color and brightness.

COLOR   When viewed through a telescope, stars have different colors. The color of a star depends on its temperature. The hottest stars are bluish white. The coolest stars are reddish-orange. "Medium-hot" stars are yellow.

BRIGHTNESS   There are two "kinds" of brightness—true brightness and apparent brightness. True brightness depends on size and temperature. The bigger and hotter an object is, the brighter it will actually be.

Apparent brightness depends mostly on distance. For example, a dim light that is close can seem brighter than a bright light that is farther away. Thus, a dim star that is close to Earth will appear brighter than a bright star that is farther away.

Star brightness is called **magnitude** [MAG-nuh-tood]. The true brightness of a star is called **absolute** [AB-suh-loot] **magnitude**. But, this is not the brightness we see when we look up at the stars. The stars that appear brightest are those closest to Earth. This brightness is called **apparent** [uh-PER-unt] **magnitude**.

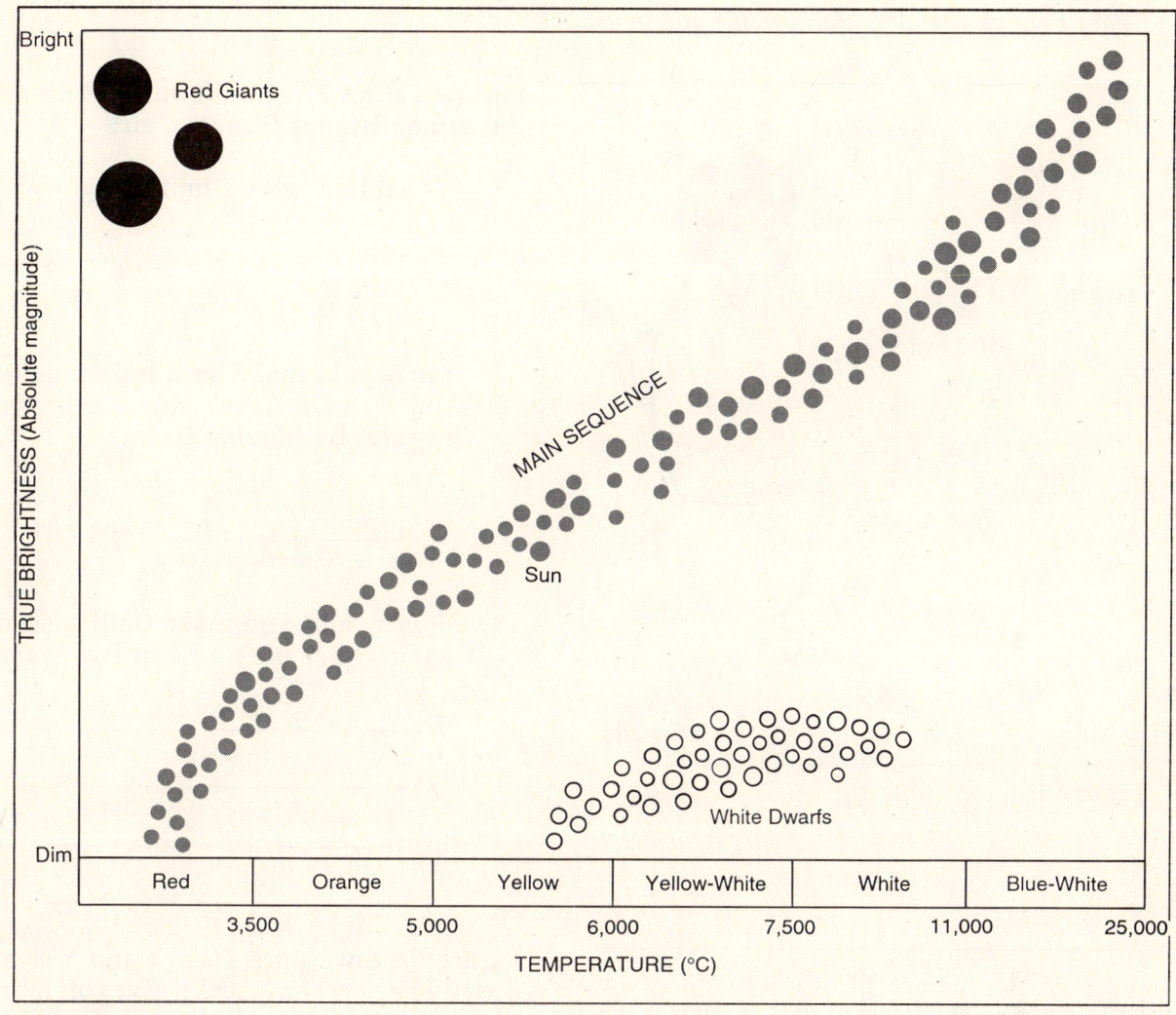

Figure A

Look at Figure A. For the stars in the main sequence, the brighter a star is, the hotter it is as well. There is a relationship between the color of a star and its brightness.

The scientists who study stars have determined that while stars are <u>not</u> alive they <u>do</u> have a life cycle similar to the life cycle of people. When stars are "born," they are dim, cool, and red. As stars age, they get brighter and hotter.

The place of a star on the main sequence is determined by its age. The stars in the bottom left corner are the youngest and the stars in the upper right corner are the oldest.

When stars get very old, they stay very bright, but they get much cooler and larger. They become red giants. Red giants are very old stars.

Some red giants, the smaller ones, eventually shrink and get dimmer, but they get whiter as well. They become white dwarfs.

Therefore, where a star is on this graph tells us how old the star is.

155

Study Figures B and C. Answer the questions.

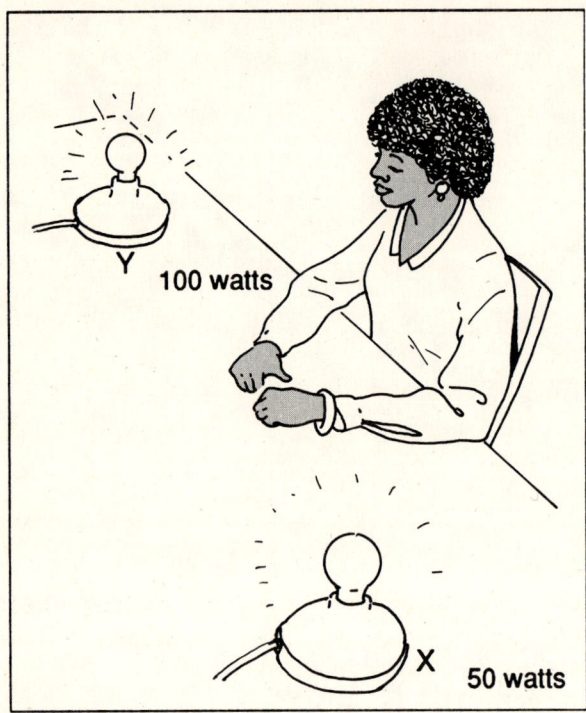

Figure B

Figure B shows two light bulbs. Both are the same distance from the girl.

1. Which bulb glows more brightly?

   _____
           X, Y

2. You would make both bulbs seem

   brighter by moving them

   _____ the girl.
   closer to, farther away from

3. How would you make bulb X seem as bright as bulb Y? List two ways.

   a) _____

   _____

   b) _____

   _____

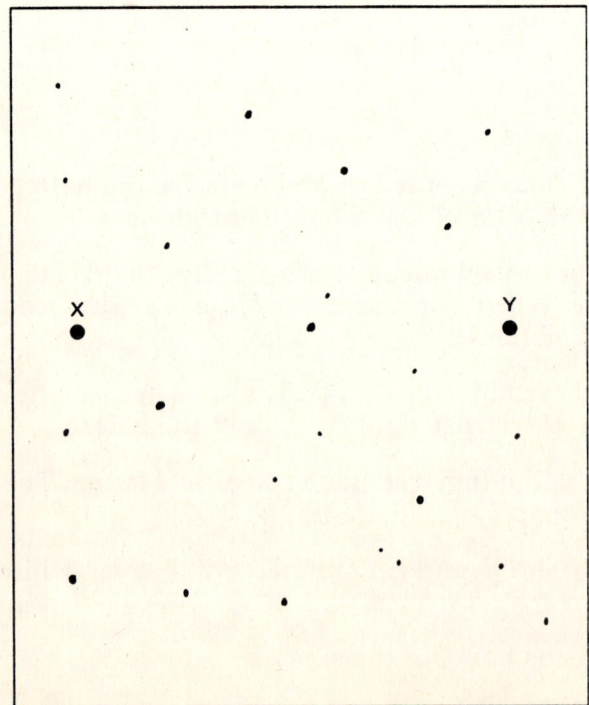

Figure C

Figure C shows stars. Stars X and Y seem equally bright. Yet, X really gives off more light than Y.

4. Which star is farther away?

   _____
           X, Y

5. Which star is closer?_____
                        X, Y

MATCHING

Match each term in Column A with its description in Column B. Write the correct letter in the space provided.

Column A

_____ 1. star color

_____ 2. true brightness

_____ 3. red giants

_____ 4. apparent brightness

_____ 5. the sun

Column B

a) a yellow star

b) stars not on the main sequence

c) depends on temperature

d) absolute magnitude

e) depends on distance

FILL IN THE BLANK

Complete each statement using a term or terms from the list below. Write your answers in the spaces provided. Some words may be used more than once.

blue-white	absolute magnitude	yellow
temperature	the sun	distance
red giants	starlight	hot gases
		star

1. Stars are made up of very_____ .

2. Apparent brightness depends mostly on_____ .

3. The color of the hottest stars is _____ .

4. Large, cool stars that are not on the main sequence are _____.

5. "Medium-hot" stars are _____ .

6. Star color depends mostly on _____ .

7. _____ is the light given off by stars.

8. The brightest star in our sky is _____ .

9. _____ brightness depends on size and temperature.

10. The true brightness of a star is called _____ .

The list on the left contains words that you have used in this Lesson. Find and circle each word where it appears in the box. The spellings may go in any direction": up, down, left, right, or diagonally.

STARLIGHT
APPARENT
BRIGHTNESS
TEMPERATURE
RED GIANT
SUN
MAGNITUDE
DISTANCE
COLOR
ABSOLUTE

```
P  R  E  A  L  F  C  O  N  T  E  R
S  A  T  T  N  A  I  G  D  E  R  N
M  O  U  S  E  D  O  O  R  M  A  T
A  L  L  W  E  R  T  Y  O  P  S  H
G  R  O  A  N  I  W  A  S  E  L  G
N  A  S  A  L  C  O  L  O  R  X  I
I  M  B  S  O  L  U  R  E  A  E  L
T  I  A  P  P  A  R  E  N  T  O  R
U  N  D  E  R  O  V  E  R  U  P  A
D  I  S  T  A  N  C  E  A  R  S  T
E  X  B  R  I  G  H  T  N  E  S  S
```

How do stars get their energy?

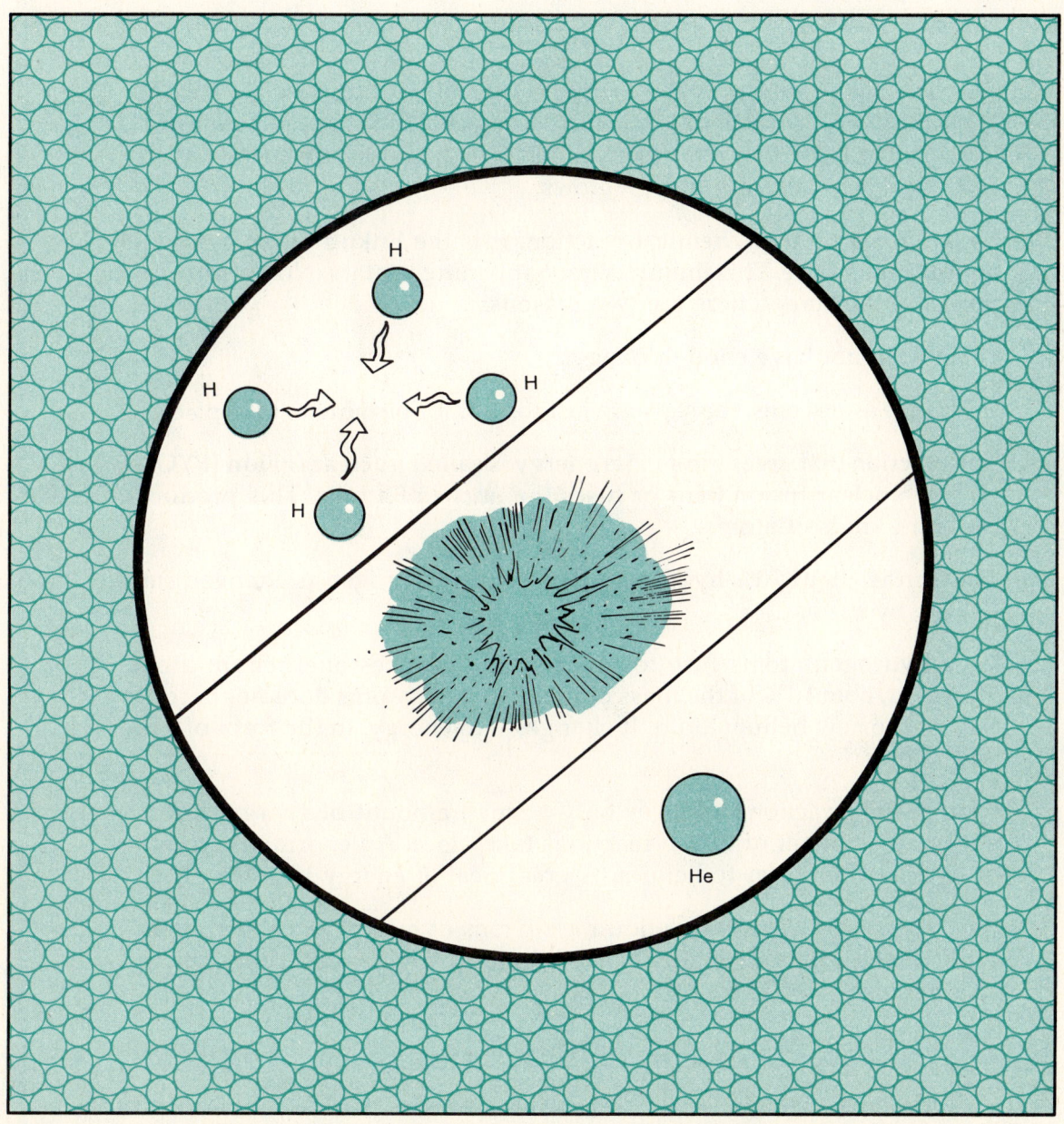

fusion [FYOO-zhun]:   joining together of hydrogen atoms to form helium atoms

LESSON 26 | How do stars get their energy?

What are stars? Most people would say "balls of burning gases." Well, this is not entirely correct. Stars are made up of gases. But they are not burning. They are glowing. The gases give off light because they are so hot. In fact, anything that is hot enough glows.

Burning is a kind of chemical reaction. It is the linkup of oxygen with another substance. This linkup is not happening in stars. No burning can take place in stars. There are two reasons:

• Stars do not have enough oxygen.

• Strange as it seems, the stars are just too hot for burning to take place.

The reaction that gives the sun its energy is called **nuclear fusion** [FYOO-zhun]. Nuclear fusion joins or fuses the nuclei of atoms. This produces different kinds of atoms.

The Sun is about 70% hydrogen. Part of this hydrogen is changed into helium by fusion.

Four hydrogen atoms fuse together. This produces one helium atom. However, about 1% of the mass of the hydrogen atoms does not become part of the new helium atom. It changes into energy, in the form of heat and light.

Each fusion reaction produces only a small amount of energy. But an enormous number of fusion reactions take place. An enormous amount of hydrogen changes to helium. A great deal of energy is given off.

Every second, about 500 million metric tons of hydrogen change to 495 million metric tons of helium. The remaining 5 million metric tons change to a huge amount of energy.

This is a nuclear equation.

$$4\ H \xrightarrow{\text{Temperature of millions of degree}} He + energy$$

It tells us that four atoms of hydrogen fuse to form one atom of helium—plus ENERGY

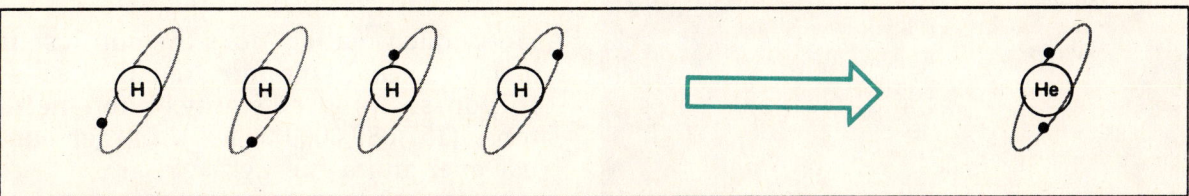

Figure A

Where does this energy come from?

Follow the explanation step-by-step.

- The atomic mass of hydrogen is 1.0081.

- The atomic mass of helium is 4.0039.

Four hydrogen atoms have a mass of 4.0324 atomic mass units (a.m.u.)

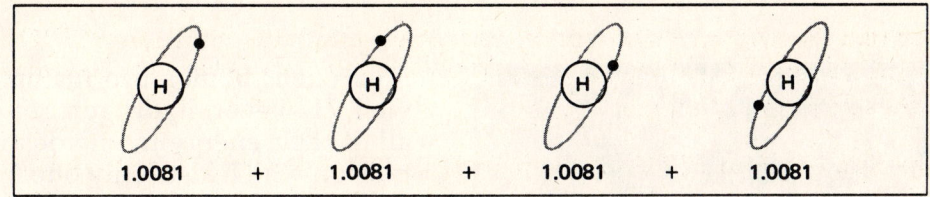

1.0081   +   1.0081   +   1.0081   +   1.0081

Figure B   4 × 1.0081 = 4.0324 a.m.u.

One helium atom has a mass of 4.0039

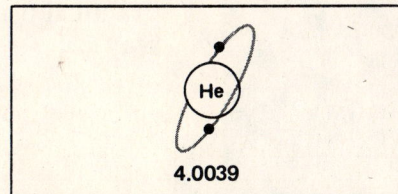

4.0039

Figure C

We see that one helium atom weighs 0.0285 less than four hydrogen atoms.

$$\begin{array}{r} 4.0324 \text{ a.m.u.} \\ -\ 4.0039 \text{ a.m.u.} \\ \hline 0.0285 \text{ a.m.u.} \end{array}$$

- It is this 0.0285 a.m.u. of matter that changes to energy.

- This reaction takes place trillions and trillions of times each second and powers stars.

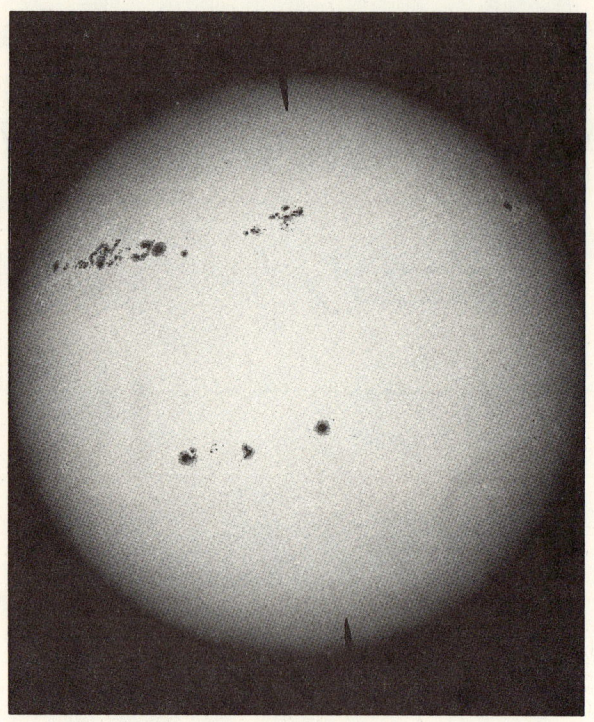

Figure D *Fusion takes place inside the sun's center.*

Talk about diets! Every second, 5 million tons of the sun's hydrogen change to energy.

This means that the sun loses 5 million metric tons of mass every second.

How much matter does the sun lose in just one year? One hundred fifty seven trillion, six hundred eighty billion metric tons. (157,680,000,000,000). Larger stars use even more energy!

Will the sun ever be used up? Yes, but not for a long, long time. The sun is so huge that it will keep on giving off heat and light for at least another billion years.

Hydrogen bombs use fusion energy as well. However, hydrogen bombs release all of their energy in one destructive explosion which lasts only one millionth of a second.

Scientists are trying to create reactors which use fusion energy to produce electricity. They have had some success, but practical uses of fusion energy are a long way off.

Figure E *Hydrogen bomb*

FILL IN THE BLANK

Complete each statement using a term or terms from the list below. Write your answers in the spaces provided.

burning   four   oxygen
helium   nuclear   energy
hydrogen   one   fusion
chemical   nuclei   light

1. Burning is a _____ reaction in which _____

   links up with another substance.

2. The energy that powers stars is not caused by _____ .

3. Stars get their energy from _____ reactions.

4. The kind of nuclear reaction that gives stars their energy is called _____.

5. Fusion joins the _____ of atoms.

6. The sun is made up mostly of _____ .

7. Fusion on the sun joins atoms of hydrogen. _____ hydrogen

   atoms fuse to form _____ atom of helium.

8. _____ is nearly four times heavier than hydrogen.

9. About 1% of the mass of the hydrogen atoms does not become helium atoms. It

   changes to _____ .

10. Anything that becomes hot enough gives off _____ .

MATCHING

Match each term in Column A with its description in Column B. Write the correct letter in the space provided.

	Column A	Column B
_____	1. fuse	a) give the sun its energy
_____	2. fusion reactions	b) nearly four times heavier than hydrogen
_____	3. hydrogen	c) about 75% of the sun
_____	4. sun	d) join
_____	5. helium	e) a star

WORD SCRAMBLE

Below are several scrambled words you have used in this Lesson. Unscramble the words and write your answers in the spaces provided.

1. SIFONU   _____

2. MILUHE   _____

3. GEENYR   _____

4. RANLUCE   _____

5. GRODHENY   _____

What are constellations? 27

constellation [kon-stuh-LAY-shun]: a group of stars that form a pattern
North Star: Polaris, the star above the north pole
Pole Star: Polaris, the star above the north pole

LESSON 27 | What are constellations?

Have you ever looked at the Big Dipper in the sky? With a little practice, it is fairly easy to find the stars that make up the Big Dipper. Why is this so?

There are seven stars that make up the Big Dipper. These stars form a pattern. Every night, when you look up into the sky, you can see this same pattern. People are good at learning patterns and then recognizing these patterns.

In ancient times, people divided the stars in the sky into different groups called **constellations** [kon-stuh-LAY-shuns]. Each constellation formed a pattern. Different societies had divided the stars up differently. The patterns reminded them of people, animals or things in their world. People would name the constellations after the things the constellations reminded them of. For example, Orion is a group of stars that reminded the ancient Greeks of Orion, the Hunter.

Astronomers today have divided the sky into 88 constellations. Every star in the sky is part of some constellation although only the brightest stars are used to form the patterns the constellation is named after. Astronomers use the names of constellations to help keep track of the stars in the sky.

The stars in a constellation look like they are close to each other as we look at them from earth. However, that does not mean that they really are close to each other. The stars in a constellation are not all the same distance from us. Some stars in a constellation are much closer to us than the other stars in the same constellation.

Figure A   *Orion*

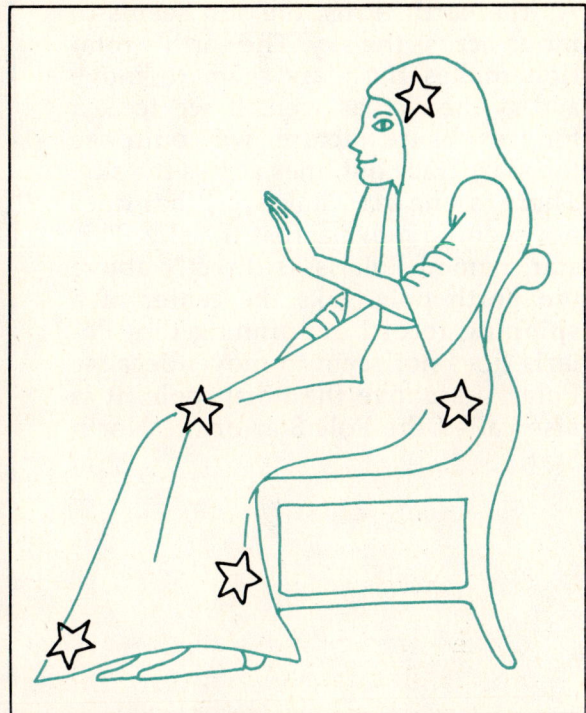

Figure B   *Casseopia*

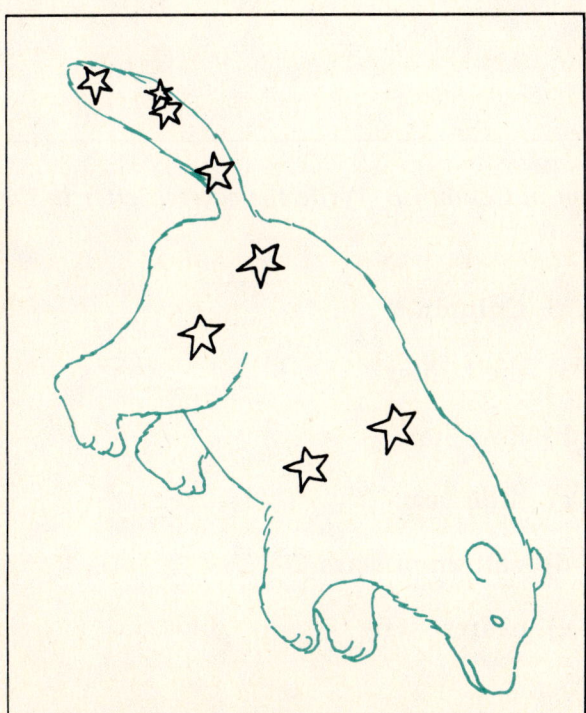

Figure C   *Ursa Major, the great bear*

Figure D   *Ursa Minor, the little bear*

THE NORTH STAR

The earth, you know, rotates on its axis. As the earth turns, the sun seems to move across the sky. The earth's rotation makes the stars seem to move across the sky as well. If we took a long exposure picture, we could see the stars trace out lines across the sky. There is one star, however, that does not seem to move across the sky. This star, named Polaris, is directly above the north pole. Like the center of a spinning record or spinning top, Polaris does not seem to move. Because Polaris is above the north pole, it is also called the Pole Star or the North Star.

Figure E

MATCHING

Match each term in Column A with its description in Column B. Write the correct letter in the space provided.

Column A	Column B
_____ 1. constellation	a) the hunter
_____ 2. Orion	b) Pole Star
_____ 3. Polaris	c) little bear
_____ 4. sun	d) pattern of stars
_____ 5. Ursa Minor	e) nearest star

FILL IN THE BLANK

Complete each statement using a term or terms from the list below. Write your answers in the spaces provided. Some words may be used more than once.

stars   patterns   look
Orion   rotates   distance
sun   constellations   North Star
Casseopia   Pole Star   Polaris
north pole

1. People are good at learning to recognize _____ .

2. A long time ago people divided the stars into groups called _____ .

3. A constellation is made up of a group of _____ .

4. _____ and _____ are constellations.

5. The stars in a constellation _____ as if they are close to each other.

6. The stars in a constellation are not all the same _____ from us.

7. The Earth _____ on its axis.

8. Because the Earth rotates, the _____ and _____ seem to move across the sky.

9. _____ does not seem to move across the sky because it is above the _____ .

10. Polaris is also known as the _____ or the _____ .

REACHING OUT

How could Polaris be useful to a person who is lost? (Hint: why is Polaris called the North Star?) _____

_____

_____

_____

SCIENCE *EXTRA*

Aerospace Technician

Neil Armstrong's "one small step for man, one giant leap for mankind" was not the achievement of just one man. Instead, his first step onto the moon's surface was the result of the labors of thousands and thousands of people. Many of those people were aerospace technicians.

Aerospace technicians built the Saturn 5 rocket which launched Armstrong into space. The technicians also built the capsule and lunar lander that carried him to the moon. They even made the space suit that he wore as he made his historic step.

Aerospace technicians build space probes, satellites, spacecraft and any other equipment that is being used in space.

The conditions in space are so severe that space equipment must be made specifically for these conditions. Even something as simple as a screw must be made of special materials to survive the conditions of outer space.

The equipment aerospace technicians make is very, very complicated.

Therefore, they take special care to make sure that the equipment they make is not defective. If something does not work the way it is supposed to, millions of dollars (even the lives of astronauts) could be lost. For this reason, aerospace technicians are very detail oriented. All work is checked and rechecked to make sure that no mistakes are made.

If, when the equipment is launched, everything functions properly, (which it usually does) aerospace technicians can be proud of the job they have done. All their hard work has paid off.

Aerospace technicians may either work for government agencies like NASA or for private aerospace companies. If you would like to be an aerospace technician, you should study math and science in school. After graduating from high school. you could either go to college and major in science or engineering or go to a technical school.

Aerospace engineering is a career with both personal and financial rewards. It may be the career for you.

What are galaxies?

28

elliptical galaxy: spherical or flattened disk-shaped galaxy
galaxy [GAL-uhk-see]:   large group of stars
irregular galaxy: galaxy with no definite shape
Milky Way galaxy: the galaxy in which the sun is located
spiral galaxy: galaxy with a thick center and flattened arms

LESSON 28 | What are galaxies?

Look up at the sky on a clear night. How many stars can you see? Take a guess. One hundred? One thousand? One million? Without a telescope, about 5,000 stars are visible from Earth. That is, from the entire Earth! Not just from your back yard.

Through a powerful telescope, millions of individual stars can be seen. Does this mean that most of the stars are visible through a telescope? Not at all. There are more stars than we could ever hope to count. There may even be an infinite number of stars.

Stars are not just scattered throughout space. They are sort of bunched together in very large groups or systems, called **galaxies** [GAL-uhk-seez]. Each galaxy contains hundreds of millions of stars. And the galaxies are millions of light-years apart.

There are three main types of galaxies—spiral, elliptical, and irregular.

A **spiral galaxy** looks something like a giant pinwheel. It has a thick center and several "arms" that spiral around the center. The planet Earth is located in a spiral galaxy—the **Milky Way galaxy**. Our sun is one of more than 100 billion stars in this galaxy.

An **elliptical galaxy** looks something like the lens of a magnifying glass. It has no arms, and most of the stars are concentrated near its center.

Irregular galaxies have no definite shape.

Figure A *Spiral galaxy*

Most galaxies are spiral galaxies. Our solar system is in the spiral galaxy called the Milky Way. We are one of the many stars in one of the arms of the Milky Way. We can't take a picture of the entire Milky Way, because we are <u>inside</u> it. However, if you go far away from city lights and look up at a very clear, very dark sky, you can see a band across the sky that glows faintly. That glow is from millions and millions of stars in the Milky Way that are too faint to see.

Figure B *Elliptical galaxy*

Elliptical galaxies look like a ball that has been squished. The stars in elliptical galaxies are usually older than the stars in spiral galaxies. Therefore, elliptical galaxies are usually not as bright as spiral galaxies.

Figure C *Irregular galaxy*

Irregular galaxies are the least common type of galaxy. The stars in an irregular galaxy are not arranged evenly so irregular galaxies have no definite shape. Irregular galaxies are smaller and fainter than the other kinds of galaxies.

Figure D

While studying galaxies, Astronomer Edwin Hubble discovered that all galaxies are moving away from each other. This means that the galaxies used to be much closer to each other. At some point a long, long time ago, everything in the universe must have been together at the same place.

Many scientists now believe that about 15 billion years ago, the universe came into being in what scientists call the big bang. This cosmic explosion created all the matter in the universe and the force of the explosions sent the matter off in all directions.

The forces that would have been acting very early in the universe are very different from what we experience in our everyday lives. As a result, scientists do not completely understand how the universe began. There is still much more to learn.

TRUE OR FALSE

In the space provided, write "true" if the sentence is true. Write "false" if the sentence is false.

_____ 1. Scientists know how many stars there are in the universe.

_____ 2. Spiral galaxies are the most common kind of galaxy.

_____ 3. The Milky Way is an elliptical galaxy.

_____ 4. Irregular galaxies have a definite shape.

_____ 5. The sun is in the Milky Way galaxy.

_____ 6. You can see the glow of the Milky Way on a clear night.

_____ 7. Spiral galaxies are shaped like a pinwheel.

_____ 8. Galaxies are moving towards each other.

_____ 9. Scientists think that a big bang created the universe.

_____ 10. Scientists know exactly how the universe began.

MATCHING

Match each term in Column A with its description in Column B. Write the correct letter in the space provided.

Column A

_____ 1. Edwin Hubble

_____ 2. irregular galaxies

_____ 3. spiral galaxies

_____ 4. elliptical galaxies

_____ 5. Milky Way

Column B

a) our galaxy

b) studied galaxies

c) most common galaxies

d) least common galaxies

e) shaped like a flattened ball

WORD SEARCH

The list on the left contains words that you have used in this Lesson. Find and circle each word where it appears in the box. The spellings may go in any direction: up, down, left, right, or diagonally.

STAR
GALAXY
ELLIPTICAL
SPIRAL
CONSTELLATION
BIG BANG
SUN
FUSION
SOLAR
MAGNITUDE

S	T	G	I	A	N	I	T	W	T	E	D
S	T	A	R	S	W	I	L	L	A	R	D
E	L	L	I	P	T	I	C	A	L	N	O
V	A	A	R	I	K	E	O	W	H	R	E
E	W	X	O	R	S	U	N	T	E	L	E
F	L	Y	V	A	D	S	S	I	O	N	S
M	U	F	N	L	I	K	T	A	R	T	O
A	W	S	I	L	T	F	E	N	I	H	D
G	S	T	E	L	L	H	L	F	I	S	E
I	F	C	O	N	E	S	L	T	I	A	H
B	U	E	D	S	O	L	A	R	E	E	E
C	S	M	A	G	N	I	T	U	D	E	W
M	I	L	A	C	O	C	I	H	A	E	N
I	O	A	R	S	M	A	O	T	N	B	R
T	N	B	I	G	B	A	N	G	J	E	N

REACHING OUT

What force keeps all the stars in a galaxy together? Why? _____

_____

_____

METRIC-ENGLISH CONVERSIONS

	Metric to English	*English to Metric*
Length	1 kilometer = 0.621 mile (mi)	1 mi = 1.61 km
	1 meter = 3.28 feet (ft)	1 ft = 0.305 m
	1 centimeter = 0.394 inch (in)	1 in = 2.54 cm
Area	1 square meter = 10.763 square feet	$1\ ft^2 = 0.0929\ m^2$
	1 square centimeter = 0.155 square inch	$1\ in^2 = 6.452\ cm^2$
Volume	1 cubic meter = 35.315 cubic feet	$1\ ft^3 = 0.0283\ m^3$
	1 cubic centimeter = 0.0610 cubic inches	$1\ in^3 = 16.39\ cm^3$
	1 liter = .2642 gallon (gal)	1 gal = 3.79 L
	1 liter = 1.06 quart (qt)	1 qt = 0.94 L
Mass	1 kilogram = 2.205 pound (lb)	1 lb = 0.4536 kg
	1 gram = 0.0353 ounce (oz)	1 oz = 28.35 g
Temperature	Celsius = 5/9 (°F −32)	Fahrenheit = 9/5°C + 32
	0°C = 32°F (Freezing point of water)	72°F = 22°C (Room temperature)
	100°C = 212°F	98.6°F = 37°C
	(Boiling point of water)	(Human body temperature)

METRIC UNITS

The basic unit is printed in capital letters.

Length	*Symbol*
Kilometer	km
METER	m
centimeter	cm
millimeter	mm

Area	*Symbol*
square kilometer	km^2
SQUARE METER	m^2
square millimeter	mm^2

Volume	*Symbol*
CUBIC METER	m^3
cubic millimeter	mm^3
liter	L
milliliter	mL

Mass	*Symbol*
KILOGRAM	kg
gram	g

Temperature	*Symbol*
degree Celsius	°C

SOME COMMON METRIC PREFIXES

Prefix		*Meaning*
micro-	=	0.000001, or 1/1,000,000
milli-	=	0.001, or 1/1000
centi-	=	0.01, or 1/100
deci-	=	0.1, or 1/10
deka-	=	10
hecto-	=	100
kilo-	=	1000
mega-	=	1,000,000

SOME METRIC RELATIONSHIPS

Unit	*Relationship*
kilometer	1 km = 1000 m
meter	1 m = 100 cm
centimeter	1 cm = 10 mm
millimeter	1 mm = 0.1 cm
liter	1 L = 1000 mL
milliliter	1 mL = 0.001 L
tonne	1 t = 1000 kg
kilogram	1 kg = 1000 g
gram	1 g = 1000 mg
centigram	1 cg = 10 mg
milligram	1 mg = 0.001 g

SAFETY ALERT SYMBOLS

 CLOTHING PROTECTION • A lab coat protects clothing from stains. • Always confine loose clothing.

 EYE SAFETY • Always wear safety goggles. • If anything gets in your eyes, flush them with plenty of water. • Be sure you know how to use the emergency wash system in the laboratory.

 FIRE SAFETY • Never get closer to an open flame than is necessary. • Never reach across an open flame. • Confine loose clothing. • Tie back loose hair. • Know the location of the fire-extinguisher and fire blanket. • Turn off gas valves when not in use. • Use proper procedures when lighting any burner.

 POISON • Never touch, taste, or smell any unknown substance. Wait for your teacher's instruction.

 CAUSTIC SUBSTANCES • Some chemicals can irritate and burn the skin. If a chemical spills on your skin, flush it with plenty of water. Notify your teacher without delay.

 HEATING SAFETY • Handle hot objects with tongs or insulated gloves. • Put hot objects on a special lab surface or on a heat-resistant pad; never directly on a desk or table top.

 SHARP OBJECTS • Handle sharp objects carefully. • Never point a sharp object at yourself-or anyone else. • Cut in the direction away from your body.

 TOXIC VAPORS • Some vapors (gases) can injure the skin, eyes, and lungs. Never inhale vapors directly. • Use your hand to "wave" a small amount of vapor towards your nose.

 GLASSWARE SAFETY • Never use broken or chipped glassware. • Never pick up broken glass with your bare hands.

 CLEAN UP • Wash your hands thoroughly after any laboratory activity.

 ELECTRICAL SAFETY • Never use an electrical appliance near water or on a wet surface. • Do not use wires if the wire covering seems worn. • Never handle electrical equipment with wet hands.

 DISPOSAL • Discard all materials properly according to your teacher's directions.

CONSTELLATIONS

Name	Abbre-viation	Meaning	Name	Abbre-viation	Meaning
Andromeda	And	Chained Maiden	Indus	Ind	Indian
Antlia	Ant	Air Pump	Lacerta	Lac	Lizard
Apus	Aps	Bird of Paradise	Leo	Leo	Lion
Aquarius	Aqr	Water Bearer	Leo Minor	LMi	Little Lion
Aquila	Aql	Eagle	Lepus	Lep	Hare
Ara	Ara	Altar	Libra	Lib	Balance
Aries	Ari	Ram	Lupus	Lup	Wolf
Auriga	Aur	Charioteer	Lynx	Lyn	Lynx
Bootes	Boo	Herdsmen	Lyra	Lyr	Lyre
Caelum	Cae	Chisel	Mensa	Men	Table Mountain
Camelopardalis	Cam	Giraffe	Microscopium	Mic	Microscope
Cancer	Cnc	Crab	Monoceros	Mon	Unicorn
Canes Venatici	CVn	Hunting Dogs	Musca	Mus	Fly
Canis Major	CMa	Great Dog	Norma	Nor	Square (rule)
Canis Minor	CMi	Little Dog	Octans	Oct	Octant
Capricornus	Cap	Sea-goat	Ophiuchus	Oph	Serpent Bearer
Carina	Car	Keel	Orion	Orti	Hunter
Cassiopeia	Cas	Queen	Pavo	Pav	Peacock
Centaurus	Cen	Centaur	Pegasus	Peg	Flying Horse
Cepheus	Cep	King	Perseus	Per	Hero
Cetus	Cet	Whale	Phoenix	Phe	Phoenix
Chamaeleon	Cha	Chameleon	Pictor	Pic	Painter
Circinus	Cir	Compasses (art)	Pisces	Psc	Fishes
Columba	Col	Dove	Pisces Austrinus	PsA	Southern Fish
Coma Berenices	Com	Berenice's Hair	Puppis	Pup	Stern (deck)
Corona Australis	CrA	Southern Crown	Pyxis	Pyx	Compass (sea)
Corona Borealis	CrB	Northern Crown	Reticulum	Ret	Net
Corvus	Crv	Crow	Sagitta	Sge	Arrow
Crater	Crt	Cup	Sagittarius	Sgr	Archer
Crux	Cru	Cross (southern)	Scorpius	Sco	Scorpion
Cygnus	Cyg	Swan	Sculptor	Scl	Sculptor
Delphinus	Del	Dolphin	Scutum	Sct	Shield
Dorado	Dor	Goldfish	Serpens	Ser	Serpent
Draco	Dra	Dragon	Sextans	Sex	Sextant
Equuleus	Equ	Little Horse	Taurus	Tau	Bull
Eridanus	Eri	River	Telescopium	Tel	Telescope
Fornax	For	Furnace	Triangulum	Tri	Triangle
Gemini	Gem	Twins	Trigulum Australe	TrA	Southern Triangle
Grus	Gru	Crane (bird)			
Hercules	Her	Hercules	Tucana	Tuc	Toucan
Horologium	Hor	Clock	Ursa Major	UMa	Great Bear
Hydra	Hya	Water Snake (female)	Ursa Minor	UMi	Little Bear
			Vela	Vel	Sail
Hydrus	Hyi	Water Snake (male)	Virgo	Vir	Maiden
			Volans	Vol	Flying Fish
			Vulpecula	Vul	Fox

THE PLANETS

Planet	Number of Moons	Distance From Sun	Diameter	Period of Rotation	Period of Revolution
Mercury	0	57,900,000 km	4,880 km	59 days	88 days
Venus	0	108,200,000 km	12,100 km	243 days	225 days
Earth	1	149,600,000 km	12,756 km	24 hours	365 days
Mars	2	227,900,000 km	6,794 km	25 hours	687 days
Jupiter	16	778,300,000 km	143,200 km	10 hours	12 years
Saturn	18	1,427,000,000 km	120,000 km	11 hours	309 years
Uranus	15	2,870,000,000 km	51,800 km	17 hours	84 years
Neptune	8	4,497,000,000 km	49,528 km	18 hours	165 years
Pluto	1	5,900,000,000 km	3,400 km	6 days 9 hours	248 years

MASSES OF THE SUN, MOON AND THE PLANETS

Sun	2,000,000,000,000,000,000,000,000,000,000 kg
Mercury	330,000,000,000,000,000,000,000 kg
Venus	4,900,000,000,000,000,000,000,000 kg
Earth	6,000,000,000,000,000,000,000,000 kg
Moon	73,000,000,000,000,000,000,000 kg
Mars	640,000,000,000,000,000,000,000 kg
Jupiter	1,900,000,000,000,000,000,000,000,000 kg
Saturn	570,000,000,000,000,000,000,000,000 kg
Uranus	87,000,000,000,000,000,000,000,000 kg
Neptune	103,000,000,000,000,000,000,000,000 kg
Pluto	15,000,000,000,000,000,000,000 kg

MAJOR MOONS

Moon	Planet	Distance From Planet	Diameter	Period of Rotation	Period of Revolution
Moon	Earth	384,000 km	3,476 km	27 days	27 days
Phobos	Mars	9,000 km	11 km	8 hours	8 hours
Deimos	Mars	23,000 km	6 km	30 hours	30 hours
Io	Jupiter	422,000 km	3,640 km	42 hours	42 hours
Europa	Jupiter	671,000 km	3,000 km	85 hours	85 hours
Ganymede	Jupiter	1,070,000 km	5,280 km	7 days	7 days
Calisto	Jupiter	1,880,000 km	5,000 km	17 days	17 days
Tetheys	Saturn	2934,000 km	1,060 km	45 hours	45 hours
Dione	Saturn	377,000 km	1,120 km	66 hours	66 hours
Rhea	Saturn	527,000 km	1,512 km	108 hours	108 hours
Titan	Saturn	1,222,000 km	5,120 km	16 days	16 days
Iapetus	Saturn	3,561,000 km	1,460 km	79 days	79 days
Ariel	Uranus	192,000 km	1,160 km	60 hours	60 hours
Umbriel	Uranus	267,000 km	1,190 km	99 hours	99 hours
Titania	Uranus	439,000 km	1,610 km	9 days	9 days
Oberon	Uranus	587,000 km	1,750 km	13 days	13 days
Miranda	Uranus	130,000 km	320 km	34 hours	34 hours
Triton	Neptune	654,000 km	3,400 km	6 days	6 days
Nereid	Neptune	5,570,000 km	940 km	360 days	360 days
Charon	Pluto	17,500 km	750 km	6 days	6 days

PHYSICAL CONSTANTS

Astronomical Unit (AU) = 150,000,000 km
Lightyear = 9,500,000,000,000 km
Speed of Light = 300,000,000 m/s

SELECTED SPACE PROBES

Spacecraft	Country of Origin	Launch Date	Accomplishments (Highlights)
Luna 2	USSR	9/12/54	First spacecraft to reach Moon
Luna 3	USSR	10/4/57	First circumnavigation of Moon, first pictures of far side
Marina 2	USA	6/27/62	First interplanetary mission—Venus flyby
Ranger 7	USA	7/18/64	Impact with Moon, transmitted first close-up pictures
Marina 4	USA	11/28/64	First close-up pictures of Mars, measurement of atmospheric surface pressure
Luna 9	USSR	1/31/66	First successful lunar soft landing
Luna 10	USSR	3/31/66	First spacecraft in lunar orbit
Surveyor 1	USA	5/30/66	First U.S. soft landing on Moon
Lunar Orbiter 1	USA	8/10/66	First lunar orbiting survey vehicle
Venera 4	USSR	6/12/67	First data back from inside atmosphere of Venus
Marina 6	USA	2/24/69	Mars flyby, first high-resolution imaging of Mars
Venera 7	USSR	8/17/70	First data back from surface of Venus
Luna 16	USSR	9/12/70	Soft landing on Moon with return of samples to Earth
Mariner 9	USA	5/30/71	Mars orbiter, first global mapping of planet
Pioneer 10	USA	3/2/72	First Jupiter flyby
Venera 8	USSR	3/26/72	First chemical analysis of Venus' surface
Pioneer 11	USA	4/5/73	Second Jupiter flyby and first Saturn flyby
Mariner 10	USA	11/3/73	First flyby of Mercury, obtained Venus data en route
Venera 9	USSR	6/8/75	Data from surface of Venus and from orbiter
Viking 1	USA	8/20/75	First soft landing on Mars, also Mars orbiter, *in situ* analyses of surface and atmosphere
Viking 2	USA	9/9/75	Second soft landing on Mars, also Mars orbiter, *in situ* analyses of surface and atmosphere
Voyager 1	USA	8/5/77	Flybys of Saturn, Titan, many experiments
Voyager 2	USA	8/20/77	Flybys of Jupiter, Saturn, Uranus, Neptune, many experiments
Pioneer Venus Orbiter	USA	5/20/78	First radar mapping of Venus from orbit
Pioneer Venus Probe Carrier	USA	8/8/78	Atmospheric composition, radiation balance, cloud particle characteristics from four entry probes
Venera 11	USSR	9/9/78	Atmospheric and cloud composition of Venus, surface studies
Venera 13	USSR	10/30/81	Venus atmosphere and surface studies, detection of lightning discharges
Venera 15	USSR	6/2/83	Orbiting radar mapper of Venus surface topography
VEGA 1	USSR	12/15/84	Venus flyby, descent probe landing, balloon deployment plus passage through Halley coma, many experiments
VEGA 2	USSR	12/21/84	Venus flyby, descent probe landing, balloon deployment plus passage through Halley coma, many experiments
Sakigake	Japan	1/8/85	Solar wind interaction with Comet Halley
Giotto	ESA*	7/2/85	Closest approach to Halley nucleus, many experiments
Suisei	Japan	8/18/85	UV imaging of Halley hydrogen corona, comet plasma measurements
Magellan	USA	5/4/89	Radar mapping of Venus surface topography
Galileo	USA	10/18/89	Jupiter orbiter with atmospheric probe

*ESA = European Space Administration = a consortium of European countries

SPACE SHUTTLE MISSIONS

Mission	Takeoff	Landing	Crew
STS-1 Columbia	4/12/81	4/14/81	Robert Crippen, John Young
STS-2 Columbia	11/12/81	11/14/81	Joe Engle, Richard Truly
STS-3 Columbia	3/22/82	3/30/82	Jack Lousma, Gordon Fullerton
STS-4 Columbia	6/27/82	7/4/82	Tomas Mattingly, Henry Hartsfield
STS-5 Columbia	11/11/81	11/16/82	Vance Brand, Robert Overmyer, William Lenoir, Joseph Allen
STS-6 Challenger	4/4/83	4/9/83	Paul Weitz, Karol Bobko, Story Musgrave, Donald Peterson
STS-7 Challenger	6/18/83	6/24/83	Robert Crippen, Norman Thagard, John Fabian, Frederick Hauk, Sally Ride (first U.S. woman in space)
STS-8 Challenger	8/30/83	9/5/83	Richard Truly, Daniel Brandenstein, William Thorton, Guion Bluford (first U.S. African American in space), Dale Gardner
STS-9 Columbia	11/28/83	12/8/83	John Young, Brewster Shaw, Robert Parker, Owen Garriott, Byron Lichtenberg, Ulf Merbold
41-B Challenger	2/3/84	2/11/84	Vance Brand, Robert Gibson, Ronald McNair, Bruce McCandless, Robert Stewart
41-C Challenger	4/6/84	4/13/84	Robert Crippen, Francis Scobee, George Nelson, Terry Hart, James Van Hoften
41-D Discovery	8/30/84	9/5/84	Henry Hartsfield, Michael Coats, Steven Hawley, Judith Resnik, Richard Mullane, Charles Walker
41-G Challenger	10/5/84	10/13/84	Robert Crippen, Jon McBride, Kathryn Sullivan, Sally Ride, Marc Garneau (first Canadian in space), David Leestma, Paul Scully-Power
51-A Discovery	11/8/84	11/16/84	Frederick Hauck, David Walker, Anna Fisher, Joseph Allen, Dale Gardner
51-C Discovery	1/24/85	1/27/85	Thomas Mattingly, Loren Shriver, James Buchli, Elison Onizuka, Gary Payton
51-D Discovery	4/12/85	4/19/85	Karol Bobko, Donald Williams, Charles Walker, Jake Garn, Jeffrey Hoffman, David Griggs, Rhea Seddon
51-B Challenger	4/29/85	5/6/85	Robert Overmeyer, Frederick Gregory, Don Lind, Lodewijk van den Berg, Norman Thagard, William Thorton, Taylor Wang
51-G Discovery	6/17/85	6/24/85	John Creighton, Shannon Lucid, Steven Nagel, John Fabian, Daniel Bradenstein, Prince Sultan Salman al-Saud (first Arab in space)
51-F Challenger	7/29/85	8/6/85	Roy Bridges, Anthony England, Karl Henize, Story Musgrave, Gordon Fullerton, Loren Acton, John-David Bartoe
51-I Discovery	8/27/85	9/3/85	John Lounge, James van Hoften, William Fisher, Joe Engle, Richard Covey

Mission	Takeoff	Landing	Crew
51-J Atlantis	10/4/85	10/7/85	Karol Bobko, Ronald Grabe, David Hilmers, William Pailes, Robert Stewart
61-A Challenger	10/30/85	11/6/85	Henry Hatsfield, Steven Nagel, Bonnie Dunbar, James Buchli, Giuon Bluford, Ernst Messerschmid, Reinhard Furrer, Wubbo Ockles
61-B Atlantis	11/26/85	12/3/85	Brewster Shaw, Charles Walker, Rodolfo Neri (first Mexican in space), Jerry Ross, Sherwood Spring, Mary Cleave
61-C Columbia	1/12/86	1/18/86	Robert Gibson, Charles Bolden, George Nelson, Bill Nelson, Franklin Chiang-Diaz, Steven Hawley, Robert Cenker
51-L Challenger	1/28/86	*	Francis Scobee, Michael Smith, Ronald McNair, Judith Resnik, Ellison Onizuka, Gregory Jarvis, Christa McAuliffe
STS-26 Discovery	9/29/88	10/3/88	Frederick Hauck, Richard Covey, David Hilmers, George Nelson, John Lounge
STS-27 Atlantis	12/3/88	12/6/88	Robert Gibson, Guy Gardner, Richard Mullane, Jerry Ross, William Shepard
STS-29 Discovery	3/13/89	3/18/89	Michael Coats, John Blaha, James Buchli, Robert Springer, James Bagian
STS-30 Atlantis	5/4/89	5/8/89	David Walker, Ronald Grabe, Mary Cleave, Norman Thagard, Mark Lee
STS-28 Columbia	8/8/89	8/13/89	Brewster Shaw, Richard Richards, David Leestma, James Adamson, Mark Brown
STS-34 Atlantis	10/18/89	10/23/89	Donald Williams, Michael McCulley, Shannon Lucid, Ellen Baker, Franklin Chang-Diaz
SS-33 Discovery	11/22/89	11/27/89	Frederick Gregory, John Blaha, Manley Carter, Story Musgrave, Katherine Thorton
STS-32 Columbia	1/9/90	1/20/90	Daniel Brandenstein, Bonnie Dunbar, James Wetherbee, Marsha Ivins, David Low
STS-36 Atlantis	2/28/90	3/4/90	John Creighton, John Casper, David Hilmers, Richard Mullane, Pierre Thuot
STS-31 Discovery	4/24/90	4/29/90	Loren Shriver, Charles Bolden, Steven Hawley, Bruce McCandless, Kathryn Sullivan
STS-41 Discovery	10/6/90	10/10/90	Richard Richards, Robert Cabana, William Shepard, Bruce Melnick, Thomas Akers
STS-38 Atlantis	11/15/90	11/20/90	Richard Covey, Frank Culberson, Robert Springer, Carl Meade, Charles Gemar
STS-35 Columbia	12/02/90	12/10/90	Vance Brand, Guy Gardner, Jeffrey Hoffman, John Lounge, Robert Parker, Samuel Durrance, Ronald Parise
STS-37 Atlantis	4/5/91	4/11/91	Steven Nagel, Kenneth Cameron, Jerry Ross, Jay Apt, Linda Godwin

* Exploded after takeoff killing crew

GLOSSARY/INDEX

absolute [AB-suh-loot] **magnitude:** true brightness of a star, 154

action: a force, 28

aphelion [af-FEEL-yun]: point in the earth's orbit where the earth and sun are the farthest apart, 72

apogee [AP-uh-jee]: point at which the moon is farthest from the earth, 94

apparent [uh-PER-unt] **magnitude:** brightness a star seems to have, 154

asteroids [AST-uh-roydz]: large chunks of rock that orbit the sun, 126

astronomer [uh-STRON-uh-muhr]: scientist who studies heavenly bodies, 2

astronomical [as-truh-NOM-ih-kul] **unit:** distance between the Earth and Sun; 150,000,000 kilometers, 20

astronomy [uh-STRON-uh-mee]: study of heavenly bodies, 2

chromosphere [KROH-muh-sfeer]: layer of the sun's atmosphere above the photosphere, 134

constellation [kon-stuh-LAY-shun]: a group of stars that form a pattern, 166

corona [kuh-ROH-nuh]: outer layer of the sun's atmosphere, 106, 134

craters [KRAY-turz]: round holes on the moon's surface, 84

dehydrated [dee-HY-drayt-ed]: an item in which water has been removed, 48

direct rays: light rays that hit the earth straight on, 78

ellipse [uh-LIPS]: oval-shaped, 72

elliptical galaxy: spherical or flattened disk-shaped galaxy, 172

environment [in-VY-run-ment]: the surroundings that living things live in, 46

equinox [EE-kwuh-nahks]: day on which the sun shines directly on the equator, 60

fusion [FYOO-zhun]: joining together of hydrogen atoms to form helium atoms, 160

galaxy [GAL-uhk-see]: large group of stars, 172

gas giants: planets that are large and primarily composed of gases, 146

gravity [GRAV-uh-tee]: force of attraction that exists between all objects in the universe, 75

high tide: time of high water level, 118

indirect rays: light rays that do not hit the earth straight on, 78

inner planets: the four planets closest to the sun, 138

international date line: imaginary line that runs north and south and separates one day from the next, 68

irregular galaxy: galaxy with no definite shape, 172

light-year: the distance that light travels in one year, 20

low tide: time of low water level, 118

lunar: moon, 84

lunar eclipse: passing of the moon through the earth's shadow, 112

magnitude [MAG-nuh-tood]: star brightness, 154

maria [MAHR-ee-uh]: broad, flat plains on the moon, 84

meteorite [MEE-tee-or-ite]: piece of rock or metal that hits the earth's surface, 84

meteoroid [MEE-tee-or-oyd]: piece of rock or metal that orbits the sun, 126

Milky Way galaxy: the galaxy in which the sun is located, 172

neap [NEEP] **tide:** tide that is not as high or low as normal tides, 121

Northern Hemisphere: the part of the earth north of the equator, 56

North Star: Polaris, the star above the north pole, 168

orbit: curved path of the one object around another object in space, 126

parallax [PAR-uh-laks]: shift of position an object seems to have when it is seen from two different points, 24

perigee [PER-uh-jee]: point at which the moon is closest to the earth, 94

perihelion [per-uh-HEEL-yun]: point in the earth's orbit where the earth and sun are the closest, 72

phases [FAYZ-uz]: changing shapes of the moon, 98

photosphere [FOH-tuh-sfeer]: inner layer of the sun's atmosphere, 132

Pole Star: Polaris, the star above the north pole, 168

prime meridian [muh-RID-ee-un]: imaginary line that runs north and south through Greenwich, England, 64

radio telescope: telescope that can receive radio waves from sources in space, 8

reaction: an opposing force that balances an action, 28

reflecting [rih-FLEKT-ing] **telescope**: telescope that uses a concave mirror to collect light and produce an enlarged image, 8

refracting [rih-FRAKT-ing] **telescope**: telescope that uses convex lenses to collect light and produce an enlarged image, 8

revolution [reh-vuh-LOO-shun]: the traveling of an object around another object, 52

rotation [roh-TAY-shun]: the spinning of an object on its axis, 52

satellite [SAT-uh-lite]: natural or artificial object orbiting a body in space, 5, 34, 126

solar eclipse [SOH-ler uh-CLIPS]: passing of the moon between the earth and the sun, 104

solstice [SAHL-stis]: day on which the North Pole points toward or away from the sun, 58

Southern Hemisphere: the part of the earth south of the equator, 56

space probe: a machine that is sent from Earth to study other objects in space, 36

Space Shuttle: reusable space vehicle, 40

spectroscope [SPEK-truh-skohp]: an instrument used to study the light coming from an object, 14

spectrum: bands of different colors of light, 14

spiral galaxy: galaxy with a thick center and flattened arms, 172

spring tide: tide that is higher and lower than normal tides, 121

telescope: an instrument that gathers and magnifies light; used to study the heavens, 8

terrestrial [tuh-RES-tree-uhl] **planets**: planets that are similar to Earth in their size and composition, 138

tide: daily change of the level of ocean water, 118

time zone: part of the Earth where it is the same time; the Earth has 24 time zones, 64

universe [YOO-nuh-vurs]: everything that exists, 2

waning [WAYN-ing]: after the full moon; as the visible part of the moon decreases, 99

waxing: after a new moon; as the visible part of the moon increases, 99